D1716252

NOT JUST PUMPING IRON

On the Psychology of Lifting Weights

ABOUT THE AUTHOR

Edward W.L. Smith, Ph.D. is a clinical psychologist in Atlanta, Georgia. His professional time is divided among the independent practice of psychotherapy, the training of psychotherapists, and writing. Dr. Smith holds an Adjunct Professorship at Georgia State University. Since 1971 he has traveled widely as a lecturer and seminar leader. Dr. Smith lives with his wife and his teenaged daughter and son. His hands have borne the callouses of the barbell for more than fifteen years.

NOT JUST PUMPING IRON

On the Psychology of Lifting Weights

By

EDWARD W. L. SMITH, PH.D.

CHARLES C THOMAS • PUBLISHER
Springfield • Illinois • U S A

Published and Distributed Throughout the World by
CHARLES C THOMAS • PUBLISHER
2600 South First Street
Springfield, Illinois 62794-9265

© *1989 by* CHARLES C THOMAS • PUBLISHER
ISBN 0-398-05544-0
Library of Congress Catalog Card Number: 88-27569

With THOMAS BOOKS *careful attention is given to all details of manufacturing
and design. It is the Publisher's desire to present books that are satisfactory as to their
physical qualities and artistic possibilities and appropriate for their particular use.*
THOMAS BOOKS *will be true to those laws of quality that assure a good name
and good will.*

Printed in the United States of America
Q-R-3

Library of Congress Cataloging in Publication Data

Smith, Edward W.L., 1942-
    Not just pumping iron: on the psychology of
lifting weights/by Edward W.L. Smith.
        p.   cm.
    Bibliography: p.
    Includes index.
    ISBN 0-398-05544-0
    1. Weight lifting—Psychological aspects. I. Title.
GV546.4.P78S64 1989
796.4'1'019—dc19   88-27569
                                                        CIP

To my father, Dr. Edward H. Smith:

I watched you train and I watched you compete.
Then, when I was ready, you placed a barbell
in my hands.

Lifting weights is the Hatha Yoga of the West.

—Edward W.L. Smith

INTRODUCTION

ONE DAY, during my internship, I was standing in the hall of the hospital talking with my supervisor. We were waiting for someone, and in our chatting we arrived at the topic of lifting weights. When I told my supervisor that I had lifted in high school and college, and from time to time since then, he said something which created a ripple which went to some deep place inside me. What he said was, "Think of all those hours you wasted lifting weights. Just think what you could have done if you had used that time to read and study or something." That was twenty years ago, or more, so the wording may not be accurate. But, that was the gist of what he said. I don't recall what I replied, but I remember that that ripple of soul searching spread within me. After long and deep consideration I have come to regard my many hours with the barbells as well spent. I have no regret for the time I have given to lifting weights. My supervisor's statement to me was a real gift, in the effect it had. It led me to question the wisdom of my choice, and to a conclusion which in a while led me back to serious lifting.

Lifting weights has had a central role in my life for about 20 years — competitive Olympic style lifting in high school and college, bodybuilding during periods in graduate school, and after several years lay off, bodybuilding again, powerlifting, and then curling competition. I have experienced competitive lifting as a teenager, as a young adult, and as an older adult, in that over-forty category given the euphemistic name "masters class." At times I have lifted for many months without having entered or even having intended on any competition. Having trained in all four of these lifting sports, and having competed in two of them, I have come to appreciate each as having something special to offer.

Those things which I have learned that lifting weights can offer, those things which are common to all forms of lifting as well as those special things that each particular form offers, has led me to the idea for the present book. I know that lifting weights can be so much more than just "pumping iron."

Lifting weights, in any of its forms, can become a vehicle for personal exploration and psychological or spiritual growth. The use of a sport for profound personal growth has been explored in writing by a number of people. The classic example is *Zen in the Art of Archery* by Eugen Herrigel (1953). Herrigel points out that although it may appear at first sight that it is degrading to associate Zen with archery, the martial arts are not just for utilitarian purposes or even esthetic purposes. His main thesis is that the martial arts are for making contact with the ultimate reality, that is, the training of the mind.

Further examples of the use of a sport for personal growth are offered by W. Timothy Gallwey (1974) in *The Inner Game of Tennis,* Timothy (sic) Gallwey and Bob Kriegel (1977) in *Inner Skiing,* Denise McCluggage (1977) in *The Centered Skier,* Michael Murphy (1972) in *Golf In the Kingdom,* Fred Rohé (1974) in his graphically beautiful and poetic *The Zen of Running,* Mike Spino (1976) in *Beyond Jogging,* and Koichi Tohei (1966) in *Aikido in Daily Life.* In addition to these books which focus on respective sports, two outstanding books have cut across specific sports lines. These are George Leonard's (1974, 1975) *The Ultimate Athlete* and Michael Murphy and Rhea White's (1978) *The Psychic Side of Sports.*

There is a relatively new area in the process of becoming defined which is known as "sports psychology." There are a few books devoted to this and a couple of journals, *Sport Psychology* and the *International Journal of Sport Psychology.* There are also two established organizations, the North American Society for the Psychology of Sport and Physical Activity, and the International Society of Sport Psychology. And, recently in the American Psychological Association, a new division has been formed, the Division of Exercise and Sport Psychology. These developments attest to the current level of growing interest.

So far, sports psychology has had as its primary focus the use of psychological methods and techniques for the enhancement of sports performance. An example is using mental rehearsal to improve a golf stroke. In addition, sports psychologists have focused their research efforts on such topics as the personality of the athlete, particularly the personality factors which distinguish the athlete from the non-athlete, the social psychology of the sports team, organizational and management issues in sports, and motivation to sustain exercise programs. But, to reiterate, **sports psychology has been mostly concerned with the improvement of sports skills through the application of psychological techniques.**

It seems clear, then, that the orientation of sports psychology, as it is usually understood, has been the use of psychology in the service of sports. The collection of books which I have listed above, however, suggests an additional orientation. This second orientation is that of sports in the service of psychological growth and personal enhancement, or to borrow a phrase from Michael Murphy (Spino, 1976), "sport as yoga." These two orientations are, in a sense, opposites. And, although often times compatible, the two orientations may in some instances conflict. That is to say, there are times when what would enhance a sports performance would be of detriment to personal growth. This will become clear in some of the material later in the book.

Recognizing this dual orientation of sports psychology, I address both in this book. Part I includes an exploration of lifting weights as a path for personal growth. In Part II I focus on the application of psychological techniques to lifting weights.

I want to share how I came to recognize this two aspect relationship between lifting weights and psychology, which parallels the dual orientation in sports psychology. In my first Olympic weightlifting contest, a state meet in 1959, I was impressed by a lifter in the weight class above me. He was a good lifter, far stronger than one would have guessed by looking at him. In fact, he seemed thin. He was oriental and a student at Iowa State University. Between his lifts he did something which was highly peculiar. Other lifters paced about or sat and talked with each other. But he went off by himself to an out of the way spot in the lifting hall and sat down with his legs crossed, and his eyes closed, and sat quietly. Remember, this was Iowa in 1959. In this context this was surely a peculiar behavior, and for an athlete in a macho sport at that. (We thought of weightlifting as macho, even though that word had not yet entered mid-Western vocabulary.) This was the first time I had witnessed Eastern meditation. Whether or not he entered an altered state of consciousness or lifted while in an altered state, I cannot say. What I do know is that I surmised that his remarkable lifting was somehow made possible by this exotic practice which he performed between lifts. This was the beginning of my education in psychological facilitation in lifting weights.

The other side of the relationship, lifting weights as a path for personal growth, took me some time to recognize. There was not a single and dramatic moment of insight as was the case in learning of psychological facilitation of lifting. Instead, I got glimpses of this over a period of years. For instance, I came to a familiarity with the "glow" following a workout. During my early years as a lifter I had bouts of depression, feeling sad, lonely, discouraged. Following a workout I most often felt a radiance about my body. This was an organismic experience involving a feeling of warmth and tingling of aliveness in my body, and a sense of optimism and well-being. A word I can apply now is "centered." My depression was temporarily vanquished and I felt a joyous peace and harmony.

Something additional happened when I became involved in Olympic weightlifting. I set some early goals such as a bodyweight press, then a bodyweight snatch. In reaching those, and further goals, I found myself not only lifting poundages that I had been unable to lift before, but setting and attaining goals of poundages which but a few months before I would not have considered in the realm of my possibility. From time to time, I made one of these previously unbelieved of lifts which, in a current popular phrase, "boggled my mind." I experienced a mysterious, ineffable feeling when I went beyond my assumed physical limits. I gradually came to recognize that the limits beyond which I was going were also mental limits, and, in fact, I learned that the mental limit was the more important one. This recurrent exceeding of my limits gave me a deep and lasting sense of self-confidence. I came to know that what I am able to do, when I am properly prepared, is often far more than I am able to guess beforehand.

So, having personally learned this dual relationship between psychology and weightlifting, I want to share what I know is possible. I intend this book for the majority of lifters, not the "professionals." I believe that **the professionals are not good models for most lifters.** The professionals and the professional-hopefuls may benefit from modeling after successful professionals, but the non-professional lifter would do well to recognize the two class system. The successful professional has a genetic advantage and has made a commitment to excellence of performance which may involve practices which are not in keeping with overall personal development. For example, the amount of time a professional must spend training far exceeds that which would fit the balanced life of a non-professional. In a seminar which I attended a few years ago, the Mr. America who was lecturing claimed that all of the top contest winners in bodybuilding used anabolic steroids. He said they had to in order to do their best and win contests in that highly competitive business. This is another example of a professional practice which is incongruent with the use of weightlifting as a path for personal growth. Not only is the training different for the professional, but there is a whole lifestyle that goes with being a professional which is different from the lifestyle of the majority of lifters. And, it is this majority to which I belong, and to which I address this book.

Joe Weider has declared that bodybuilding is the sport of the '80s. Perhaps. At any rate, the listing of weight equipped gyms in any city and the rash of relevant magazines on any well stocked magazine stand attest to the burgeoning interest. Coverage of major bodybuilding, Olympic lifting, and powerlifting events on television is further evidence that pumping iron is no longer an esoteric activity and that the weight sports have reached a heretofore unknown popularity. It is timely that there be a book which invites and guides lifters in the use of the weight sports as paths for personal growth and enrichment.

CONTENTS

Also by Edward W. L. Smith:

The Growing Edge of Gestalt Therapy (Ed.)
The Body in Psychotherapy
Sexual Aliveness
Gestalt Voices (Ed.)

NOT JUST PUMPING IRON

On the Psychology of Lifting Weights

Part I

A PSYCHOLOGICAL PERSPECTIVE ON LIFTING WEIGHTS

Chapter 1

A TYPOLOGY OF LIFTERS

IN THE EARLY days of "strongmen," the late 1800s and the early 1900s, the focus was on an exciting, if not breath-taking performance. The successful strongman had to be versatile and a good showman in order to sell tickets. These early strongmen typically would capture their audience by performing a variety of stunts, lifting an assortment of spherical barbells, dumbbells, and kettlebells in various one or two hand lifts, as well as lifting various and sundry heavy objects such as large animals, automobiles, anvils, cannon, and platforms loaded with people. They also bent and broke metal objects such as spikes, horseshoes, and chains. These feats of strength were punctuated with poses and muscle flexing, leading up to a grand finale, often involving a dangerous stunt, or at least the stunt which appeared to be the most difficult of the show. Such was the image of the modern day strongman, a versatile man of muscle who looked the part and could demonstrate his strength. Undoubtedly, it was this nineteenth century strongman who was the inspiration and the model for the burgeoning interest in weightlifting.

With growing interest in the new "physical culture," and the new popularity of dumbbells, came the beginning of specialization. The all-round strongman image began to change with several historically important events. First, came the revival of the Olympic Games in 1896. That year there were two weightlifting events, a one-hand lift and a two-hand lift. Dropped from the list of events in the 1900 Olympic Games, weightlifting was reinstated in 1904, only to be dropped again in 1908, and again left out in 1912. Thanks to the Kaiser, the world was too busy for play in 1916, so no Olympic Games were held that year. Weightlifting was restored as an Olympic event in the 1920 games. That year three lifts were contested, the one hand snatch, one hand clean and jerk, and two hands clean and jerk. In 1924, five lifts were contested, the two arm press and the two arm snatch being added to the three lifts used in 1920. As of 1928 the Olympic lifts became the two arm press, the two arm snatch, and the two arm clean and jerk, and remained so until 1972 when the press was discontinued (Gaudreau, 1975).

With the specific designation of Olympic lifts, other lifts which were contested from time to time came to be called "odd lifts." And then, in the early 1960s, three of the "odd lifts" emerged as a frequent threesome to be contested, the bench press, the squat, and the deadlift. With that, "powerlifting" was established in its own right. The first U.S. national championships were held in 1964 (Todd, 1978).

Thus, competitive lifting emerged and evolved. The other branch of the old strongman show, muscle flexing, was launched as an independent endeavor by Bernarr Macfadden in 1903 when he put on the first physique contest at the old Madison Square Garden as a promotional device for his magazine, *Physical Culture* (Gaines and Butter, 1974). In time, then, physique contests and Olympic lifting emerged as the two branches from the trunk which was the nineteenth century strongman show. Each of these branches has evolved considerably, and competitive lifting, in its evolution has branched again, with powerlifting.

Bodybuilding, Olympic lifting, and powerlifting are the contemporary forms which grew from the strongman shows of the late 1800s and early 1900s. Not only do they share a common historical root, but they share a common behavior, that of lifting weights. Some have suggested the terms weightlifting to designate competitive lifting and weight training to designate the lifting of weights for improvement of strength and physique (Rasch, 1966). This distinction calls attention to yet another use of the lifting of weights, one not involving either lifting competition or physique competition. That is lifting weights in order to gain strength to in turn improve one's performance in some other sport. This use of lifting weights is sometimes referred to by the scientifically descriptive phrase "progressive resistance exercise."

There is one more realm of lifting weights, which is physical therapy. Given that progressive resistance exercise is proven to be the most effective and most efficient way to develop muscular strength and muscular size, it has naturally found application in the rehabilitation of those needing such work. Whether through birth defect or muscular atrophy following injury or disease, progressive resistance exercise is the treatment of choice. The goal in this realm of lifting weights is to bring a person who is below normal in muscular strength or size to a normal level of strength and size. So, the goal may be the practical one of getting a weakened muscle strong, or the cosmetic one of getting a withered muscle up to normal size. I mention the physical therapy realm for two reasons. First, it is in this context that many people have been exposed to lifting weights. And second, there are a number of people who, having started with lifting for the purpose of rehabilitation, have decided after attaining their original goals to continue lifting in the sports realms.

I want to draw a distinction, then, between "softcore" and "hardcore" lifting. **Softcore lifting includes physical therapy, physical fitness, and weight training to improve one's performance in a non-lifting sport.** For the softcore lifter, the weights are usually merely a means to an end. He or she has a goal and lifting weights is a way to facilitate getting to that goal. In the case of physical therapy the aim is to go from below average to average in muscular size and strength. For the person who lifts for physical fitness, the purpose is to go from average to above average in muscular fitness. And for the athlete who uses weights as an adjunct in her or his training, the goal is to jump higher, throw farther or faster, hit harder or farther, run or swim faster, and so on. With such pragmatic goals, the softcore lifters rarely find great enjoyment or devotion to the lifting endeavor, *per se.* Such lifters may recognize that they have to lift in order to get what they want, but they probably won't feel any love for lifting.

Hardcore lifting, on the other hand, includes the weight sports: bodybuilding, Olympic lifting, powerlifting, and odd lifting. In the weightlifting sports there is a real intimacy with the weights. There is a focus of personal encounter with the weights, as well as an identification on the lifter's part with weightlifting as her or his sport. And, in each of these the lifter is training for competition, or at least the possibility of competing at some time.

The several sports of hardcore lifting share a great deal, as suggested in the preceding paragraph. Still, each of them involves some unique quality. Let's examine what is unique to each type of hardcore lifting.

The most obvious distinction is between bodybuilding and weightlifting competition. In Olympic lifting, powerlifting, and odd lifting one trains to accomplish the heaviest lifts possible in the respective events. In contrast, the bodybuilder lifts in order to develop her or his muscles for an esthetic end. So, in one case it is how much you can lift that matters, while in the other case it is how you look as result of lifting that is important.

Even among the competitive lifting sports we can see some interesting differences. All of them place a premium on strength, to be sure, but beyond this are some differences in emphasis. Odd lifting is the least organized. For the most part it consists of local events sponsored by a community gym or YMCA, and without any sanction from a governing body. The lifts which are contested are themselves not standardized and are at the whim of the sponsor. Not only are there not standard odd lifts, but the rules for judging an odd lift are usually left to the discretion of the person sponsoring the contest. Any weightlifting exercise, potentially, can be contested, and anyone can create a set of nonce rules for judging a fair lift. For example, I have competed in arm curl contests sponsored by local gym owners, a YMCA, and private promotors. Sometimes there were three judges, sometimes two. And, sometimes the rules were strict (e.g., knees locked during the lift, elbows extended fully at the start of the lift, bar remaining parallel to the floor throughout the lift, lift starting at the front judge's signal), sometimes lax (e.g., get the bar up any way you can as long as you don't move your feet or touch the back board during the lift, start the lift when you are ready). I have been in contests where the distance from the heel mark to the back board was four inches and where it was six inches. Even the equipment varies. I have competed with both a straight bar and a cambered bar. What is implied by all this is that odd lift competition is mostly for fun. It is not "serious" competition. I would be surprised to find that anyone trains just for odd lift competition. In my experience odd lifters are bodybuilders or powerlifters who on fairly short notice get together for some "friendly competition."

Since the 1960s, when powerlifting became organized and claimed the bench press, the deadlift, and the squat as its events, the two arm curl has probably been the most frequently chosen odd lift. In the case of this lift, the basic requirement is strength. With reasonably strict rules, there is little opportunity for technique variations. Therefore, coordination is not a big factor. In a 1985 *Iron Man* article I expressed my opinion that the arm curl contest is a mini-version of powerlifting. Although not as glamorous as its big brother, it doesn't involve the degree of risk of injury which is true of powerlifting. For this reason, it clearly has a place for those lifters wanting an experience in a contest of raw strength, but for whatever reasons are not up to powerlifting competition (Smith, 1985).

Powerlifting, in terms of the number of participants, is clearly the most popular form of lifting competition. In spite of its much shorter history as an organized sport, powerlifting has eclipsed Olympic lifting in this country, and others. No doubt it has won many lifters who in earlier years would have been Olympic lifters, using deadlifts and squats only as training lifts in the service of their snatches and cleans and jerks. It is the epitome of the display of raw, brute strength. And herein, may lie much of its appeal. Terry Todd (1978), an indisputable member of powerlifting's royal court, has opined that its "primitive, artless quality" is one of the characteristics which is responsible for the rapid growth of interest in the sport. In addition, I suggest that powerlifting has been aided in its growth by its sharing its competitive lifts with bodybuilders and Olympic lifters, each of whom uses some combination of bench pressing, deadlifting, and squatting in their training. At least the deadlift and the squat are common to bodybuilding, Olympic lifting, and powerlifting. The bench press is shared at least by bodybuilders and powerlifters. The thing which is unique about powerlifting is that it involves competition in those three lifts. What this means is that anyone who has tried bodybuilding or Olympic lifting has some familiarity with powerlifting. This does not work the other way around quite so well, at least in the case of Olympic lifting. It is quite rare for a bodybuilder or powerlifter to practice snatches or cleans and jerks. My guess is that many powerlifters have evolved from an earlier introduction to bodybuilding, and some from a start in Olympic lifting.

Powerlifting requires all around muscular strength. When doing the three powerlifts as exercises, using light to moderate weights, one feels them in the muscles which are the prime movers. For example, the day after doing deadlifts, muscular soreness is usually experienced in the lower and middle back, sometimes the buttocks. Similarly, with the bench press, it is in the pectorals. And, with the squat it is the quadraceps and the buttocks which are visited by next day soreness. When these same lifts are executed with near maximum poundages, the stabilizing muscles and synergistic muscles are also stressed sufficiently to become sore. I remember, clearly, my surprise when I started training with heavy weights in the deadlift and experienced next day soreness in my biceps! There are even cases of powerlifters who have torn their biceps doing that ultimate of **back** lifts.

In Olympic lifting the elements of speed and coordination figure prominently, in addition, of course, to strength. Comparing any powerlift to a snatch or a clean and jerk makes a truism out of the above statement. In addition, Olympic lifting is unique in lifting competition in so far as it involves lifting weights overhead. The snatch and the clean and jerk are movements which must be practiced. Any normal adult could perform the powerlifts or most oddlifts the first time they tried, given a light weight. Not so, with the Olympic lifts. These two lifts reflect a greater degree of refinement. Another way of saying this is to say that the Olympic lifts are not movements which are likely to be carried out in the usual course of living and working physically. A case could be made that they are in this way different from the powerlifts, in that the latter involve more natural movements of physical work. Basic movements of lifting an object off the ground, pushing, and carrying an object on one's back are expressed in the deadlift, bench press, and squat, respectively. The snatch and clean and jerk have precious little application in life.

Bodybuilding differs dramatically from competitive lifting. I use the word "dramatically" in both of its meanings. Not only is the contrast great, that is, dramatic, but competitive bodybuilding is a performing art. No less an expert than the venerable Sigmund Klein (Gaines & Butler, 1974) has declared that bodybuilding is a "very serious performance of art." Similarly, Arnold Schwarzenegger (1977) has said that posing is pure theater. Bodybuilding is athletic training with an esthetic goal. That is, the training involves the lifting of weights, but the purpose is to produce a visual effect.

The bodybuilder is a sculptor, operating upon herself or himself as the medium. The tape measure and the mirror mark progress for the bodybuilder rather than the poundages lifted. In fact, the way of going about lifting weights in bodybuilding is different from the way that they are lifted in training for competitive lifting. The bodybuilder lifts in a manner to produce a "burn" in the muscles and a maximum "pump." He or she wants to feel the burning sensation and the full engorgement of the muscle with blood. These are the two major body sensations that guide her or his efforts. This biofeedback is the major source of information that guides the bodybuilder during the actual performance of an exercise. The tape measure, quantifying the degree of muscular tumescence, and the mirror, giving visual evidence for the pump, serve as feedback as to the effectiveness of the training session. So, the bodybuilder lifts weights in a manner which produces a burn and a pump, in order to achieve growth in muscle **size.** The competitive lifter, on the other hand, lifts in a manner which leads to maximum muscular **strength.** The training routines used by these two types of lifters will, therefore, differ markedly. The amount of weight used, the number of sets of an exercise, and the number of repetitions of the movement within the set, as well as many of the exercises themselves, will differ. The competitive lifter, wanting to lift as much weight as possible learns to lift as efficiently as possible. But, the bodybuilder, in her or his seeking a burn and a pump, may intentionally lift inefficiently. That is, the bodybuilder may lift from a posture or with a movement which increases the difficulty of the lift in order to create the desired burn and pump. Consider, for example, the difference between the standing barbell curl, used in competition, and the "preacher curl," in which the specially designed bench immobilizes the upper arm at an angle which greatly increases the stress near the insertion of the biceps. The latter is a favorite with bodybuilders seeking a biceps pump.

Another interesting difference in the way that competitive lifters and bodybuilders compete is in the nature of the judgment of the contest. In lifting competition, the judgment is relatively objective, the outcome being determined by how much weight was lifted. One competitor totals 450 pounds, another 460 pounds, and the latter is the winner. Granted, there is a degree of subjectivity in judging if a lift is done in accordance with the rules. But, this is simply a pass-fail judgment, and once the lift is passed, the criterion of winning is the poundage. Compared to that, judging bodybuilding competition is highly subjective. A panel of judges will be rating each contestant on numerical scales for several attributes such as muscularity, symmetry, definition, and posing ability. These several scores, from several judges, must then be averaged to determine an overall score. An additional complication arises in that not all contests are based on the rating of the same set of attributes. For instance, some contests do not consider posing ability, while other contests weigh this highly.

Bodybuilding competition is peculiar in that what one may be judged on is one's accomplishment as a sculptor of her or his own body, relative to a more or less agreed upon "ideal" look, and one's ability to display that sculpted body in a manner judged pleasing. The more or less agreed upon ideal look has changed over the years. In earlier days of bodybuilding competition a smoother look was popular, whereas in recent years the highly chiseled or "cut" look (highly defined muscles) and high "vascularity" (prominence of veins, indicating an extremely small amount of subcutaneous fat) have been valued. In women's bodybuilding competition disagreement as to the ideal look continues to divide judges, competitors, and spectators. Two ideals, the "muscular" look and the "feminine" look, as they are usually labeled, vie for greater popularity.

The several personal paths of lifting weights include, as one dimension, the types of lifting which I have covered in the above discussion. The second dimension is that of motivation to lift. I believe that one can approach lifting weights from any one of four motives.

The first motive is one of compliance. The person so motivated believes that he or she "should" lift. The "should" comes from outside the person. In other words, this lifter lifts because of doctor's orders, pressure from family, friends, or society. Lifting is a sort of moral choice, so that by lifting this person believes he or she is being "good," and, conversely, not to lift makes her or him "bad." This lifter is living by someone else's standard, and feeling good or bad about herself or himself based on her or his degree of compliance. What this means is that the person who lifts because of a "should" is doing so to avoid disapproval. Therefore, this person will probably only lift when he or she is watched and will tend to get out of workouts when not under the surveillance of the author of the "should." This lifter identifies herself or himself by saying things such as this when leaving the gym. "I'm glad that's over. Now I can say I worked out today."

Lifting weights as a means to an end is the second motive. The lifter who lifts for this reason does so because of the following contingency: I "have to" lift in order to get what I want. So, this lifter is goal oriented. He or she wants something, and lifting is the way to get it. Lifting is the price one has to pay. The lifter who lifts from this "have to" motive probably doesn't like lifting, *per se,* and continues only as long as doing so seems to bring the goal closer. Once the goal is reached, this motive no longer serves. This is the motive of the person who lifts until the muscles, weakened from disease or accident, are restored to normal, or until he or she has gotten in shape to play a favored sport. It is also the motive of the person who competes in the weight sports in order to feel successful, to be popular, to win trophies. The key to understanding the "have to" motive is that the lifting is not done for itself, but for the attainment of something else.

In the case of the third motive to lift, lifting is done for the experience itself. In contrast to the two motives discussed above, "I should lift," and "I have to lift," this one is "I want to lift." Lifting is done for the pleasure inherent in the act itself. The act is a process, and this lifter enjoys the process of lifting weights. The two earlier motives are easier to understand, perhaps because they are more common in our experience. But, even if one has never experienced the pleasure of lifting, it may be more nearly understood by one's remembering of other situations where one played very hard, yet enjoyed the "hard work" of that play.

There can be bodily pleasure in lifting weights, undeniable by anyone who has experienced it. Arnold Schwarzenegger has even likened working out to a sexual experience. So, lifting can be experienced as sensual, enlivening, and even sexual. It can also be playful. A workout can be fun and recreational.

This third motive to lifting weights is an intrinsic motive. It comes from inside one's self and is based on the fun and good feelings which attend a workout. The person who lifts from this motive may lift for a long period of her or his life, and is likely to look forward eagerly to training sessions.

I want to identify one more motive for lifting weights, one which is less common than the others, and is rarely acknowledged. What I am referring to is lifting weights as a path of personal growth. By "personal growth" I mean more than physical development. I mean the growing which includes one's entire being. It includes those areas sometimes distinguished as physical, mental, emotional, and spiritual. In other words, I am suggesting that lifting weights can be chosen as a way of holistic development. Using the lifting of weights as the medium, one can explore one's self, come to know one's self more intimately, confront one's conflicts and fears, and grow beyond these points of conflict and fear. It can be a way of encountering one's self at many levels, and even of confronting and working with unresolved psychological issues.

I see lifting weights as a path for raising one's consciousness. The idea that sports may serve such a process has been suggested by many others. This idea is, for example, central to the work of George Leonard (1974, p. 20), as he expressed in *The Ultimate Athlete,* "...sports and physical education, reformed and refurbished, may provide us the best possible path to personal enlightenment and social transformation in this age."

The four motives to lifting weights are, then, "I should," " I have to," "I want to," and as a "path." I see a developmental order to these motives. Each one reflects a more highly developed consciousness than the previous one. Consider that "I should" reflects a position of lifting because someone else wants me to, "I have to" because I want something that lifting can lead to, and "I want to" because of intrinsic joy and pleasure. And, finally, lifting weights as a path is a way of personal growth.

These four motives for lifting weights do not always operate in pure form. In fact, it is not uncommon for a given person to lift out of some combination of two or more of these. It may be that for a given person of mixed motives, only that combination of motives provides a strong enough impetus for her or him to lift. In other cases of mixed motives it may be that there would be adequate impetus to lift even if one or more of the operating motives were not operating. In this situation the mixed motive is more than sufficient, and to use a psychological term, the lifting behavior is "overdetermined." Even in cases where there are mixed motives, overdetermined or not, we can look for the dominant or major motivation.

Now, to develop a typology of lifters we can combine the various ways of lifting weights discussed above with these dominant motives. Doing so yields a two dimensional model which can be summarized in a 4 × 6 table, as appears in Figure 1. (Odd lifting is excluded since it is not practiced exclusively.)

"A rose, is a rose, is a rose" applies to many things and to many situations. This adage does not, however, apply to lifting weights. Often, people speak or write as if "lifting weights, is lifting weights, is lifting weights." This assumption of uniformity is a myth, held mostly by people who are themselves not veterans of lifting. I have shown in the present chapter that there are four major motives for lifting, occurring alone or in combination, and that there are basically six kinds of lifting activity which may be engaged in, one at a time or in some combination. As summarized in Figure 1, this means 24 types of lifters, theoretically.

Figure 1

A Typology of Lifters

| Motives for Lifting | Softcore Lifting | | | Hardcore Lifting | | Competitive Weightlifting |
	Physical Therapy	Training for Another Sport	Physical Fitness	Bodybuilding	Powerlifting	Olympic Lifting
I Should						
I Have to						
I Want to						
Path for Personal Growth						

In reality, some combinations of motive and type of lifting may occur rarely, if at all. For example, in lifting for physical rehabilitation the usual motive would be "I should" or "I have to," and it would be more unusual to find such a lifter lifting because he or she "wanted to," let alone as a growth path. What does sometimes happen is that the motive may evolve, and the type of lifting then change in response. So, if our lifter in this example evolves to a position of lifting out of an "I want to" motive, or as a path of growth, it is probable that he or she would change to another style of lifting.

Let me return to my point. To regard all lifting as having the same meaning is in error. In place of this "uniformity assumption myth," I am suggesting that a **"psychological** specificity" attends each of the 24 types of lifting identified above. Exercise physiologists for years have been aware of a phenomenon which they term **"physiological** specificity." What this means, basically, is that a given physiological response results from a particular physical activity. Doing a particular activity leads to a particular physical conditioning, and that conditioning has a certain specificity. As muscles are used for one activity they come to adapt to that activity, but if one changes the activity of those same muscles, they must adapt again. An example within the realm of lifting is switching to a new exercise. Let's say you have been doing barbell curls. If you switch to dumbbell curls, using the same total weight, same number of sets, and same number of repetitions, which you had become accustomed to, you most likely will wake up the following day with sore biceps.

I am suggesting that there is a psychological specificity which is analogous to physiological specificity. Each of the 24 types of lifting identified in Figure 1 provides a specific experience, and each of those experiences has a specific psychological impact. **The implication of this psychological specificity is that what one gets out of lifting weights will depend both on the motive out of which he or she lifts and the style of lifting done.** Lifting as a "path" is the motive which holds the greatest potential for personal growth. It is to lifting, as a "path" that the following chapter is devoted.

Chapter 2

LIFTING WEIGHTS AS A PATH
FOR PERSONAL GROWTH

THE GREATEST potential from lifting weights lies in doing so as a path for personal growth. When one lifts from this motive some marvelous things can happen, and one can be transformed. As such, lifting becomes a "way." This idea of the path or the way begs further explanation.

In Taoist philosophy the "way" is a central concept. Through Taoist influence, particularly in China and Japan, the "way" came to have special and deep meaning. The Japanese word for this is "do," as in aikido, judo, and kendo. It can be described as the path to enlightenment, a fine-tuning of the self in harmony with the universe. The Taoist position is that eternal truths cannot be learned through direct verbal teaching, for they cannot even be put in words. Such learning must come obliquely, as through parable, metaphor, and implication. Disciplined physical activity provides the lived experience of such metaphor and implies the eternal truth. So, as one practices her or his physical discipline, he or she is immersing himself or herself in an activity which can lead to knowing and understanding life. This understanding or enlightenment cannot be gotten second hand through the words which are about someone else's experience, but only by experiencing this truth one's self. The process is unexplainable, and intuitive. The various "do"s are well-developed systems of holistic pursuit (i.e., involve all aspects of the person, physical, mental, emotional and spiritual). They provide a disciplined exposure to experiences which serve as the metaphors for enlightenment. Such experiential learning requires time; it is not through brief exposure that deep understanding comes. Reflecting this, some of the techniques of the "do"s are termed "twenty year techniques," meaning

17

that at least that long is required for their mastery. To master the entirety of a particular "do" could require much longer, even a lifetime.

In the Western world there is also attention given by some to the idea of a "path." I find part of Don Juan's discussion with Carlos Castaneda to be of particular help in adding an important perspective on the meaning of a path (Castaneda, 1968). Don Juan explains that there are many paths, so each path is only one candidate among a million. The idea is to look at several available paths, and after close and deliberate examination, to choose one. If, after traversing a path for awhile you find that it is not right for you, then abandon it, and seek another path. If a path is not right for you, you must leave it. This decision can only come through a disciplined experience with the path. The decision to keep to a particular path or abandon it must be free from fear or ambition. The important question to ask, Don Juan tells us, is: Does this path have a heart? A path with heart makes for a joyful journey. As you follow it you are at one with it and it makes you strong. A path without heart will weaken you and make you curse your life.

Applying these ideas to lifting weights, I have come to the following conclusions:

1. The lifting of weights, in its several forms, can be a path for enlightenment, a "way."
2. The amount of growth one realizes from the path of lifting weights depends on the degree of discipline and the length of time one spends on the path.
3. Lifting weights is a path particularly suited to a Western world view.
4. Lifting weights is not a path for everyone, and is of value only for those who, after traveling it for awhile, find it has "heart."

I hope that these conclusions come to have greater meaning via the material which follows in this and the succeeding chapters.

I mentioned above that the amount of growth one realizes from following the path of lifting weights depends on one's degree of discipline. Perhaps in reaction to the rigidity of Victorian morals and activities inspired by that morality, the idea of discipline has become distasteful to many. To many, discipline means forcing one's self to do something which one does not want to do. Such forcing inevitably leads to resistance, resentment, and the abandoning of the activity as soon as that seems safe. This distorted view of discipline is consistent with the "I should" motive which I discussed in Chapter 1. Another frequent confusion is between compulsion and discipline. Discipline, freely chosen, is what keeps one on the path. **Discipline means to respect the path and one's own growth enough to want to stay on it with care and attention, at times even when it is difficult.** Again, it does not mean to comply compulsively, no matter what. It means to be committed to working on one's self through the pursuit of growth-oriented experiences. Discipline is consistent, then, with the motives of "I have to in order to," and "I want to." It is a hallmark of the "path of personal growth" motive.

The disciplined lifter is careful about lifting, careful about following a schedule, careful about diet, careful about her or his form in executing an exercise. Sometimes this care means nudging one's self to go ahead and work out. It does not mean forcing! A good example of this was given by a well-known bodybuilder who stated that he never worked out when he didn't feel like it. He noted that working out when one is not in the mood means just going through the motions, and that gains are absent from such uninspired training sessions.

The value of discipline is learned through the experience of discipline. Through the disciplined following of the path of lifting weights, one can come to recognize the nature of discipline, as distinct from compulsive forcing of activity, and to truly know its value as an element of transformation.

In the far eastern Orient, the martial arts have been the predominant physical disciplines pursued for personal growth. In India, it has been Hatha Yoga. A basic and important difference between the martial arts and Hatha Yoga is that the martial arts are designed for combat; they involve physical techniques developed for self-defense. Hatha Yoga, on the other hand, is more purely a discipline for working on one's self.

Hatha Yoga is one of many forms of yoga, all of which are practiced as paths to enlightenment. Hatha Yoga is the basic yoga of physical discipline, the yoga which teaches mastery of the body. Its major focus is on the practice of progressively more difficult "asanas" or postures, and the practice of breathing techniques or "pranayama." Diet and meditation are additional aspects of the system. Through Hatha Yoga one can develop the physical health and strength to support the more advanced yogas.

Hatha Yoga is among the oldest yoga practices, dating back at least to 2500 B.C.. So, it has, through its long evolution, been keenly refined. And, it is this yoga which is best known and most widely practiced in the West.

I see an analogy between lifting weights, or, more specifically, bodybuilding, and Hatha Yoga. Bodybuilding is to the West what Hatha

Yoga is to India. Both are systems of physical practice for the development of the self. Because of its higher degree of refinement, Hatha Yoga
can be taken as a model for the disciplined physical practice of working
on one's self. It is a model for the seeking of enlightenment through experience in the flesh. As such, the weightlifter can learn much from Hatha Yoga as a model for lifting weights.

Let us look at some of the differences between Hatha Yoga and lifting
weights. As mentioned above, Hatha Yoga is of ancient origin, perhaps
well over 4000 years old. As a system, lifting weights is less than 100
years old. Most of the weightlifting movements used today were derived
from a standard set of exercises introduced by Theodor Siebert in Germany in 1907 (Rasch, 1966). So, in comparison, weightlifting is an in-
fant. It has hardly begun to realize its potential as a path for enlightenment. In this infantile stage, weightlifting is, for most lifters, simply a
sport or simply a means to get "big and strong." Very few even recognize
that lifting can be a disciplined path leading to the experience of eternal
truths.

Traditionally, Hatha Yoga is taught through the personal instruction
of a guru. The guru is highly developed, highly evolved. Too often, in
contrast, weightlifting is learned by trial and error and watching others,
through a book, or from an "instructor" of dubious credentials. There is
not a tradition of esteemed teachers in weightlifting, only a few good instructors, often not well-known. The majority of instructors, in my experience, are not well trained, experienced, or even very knowledgeable, let alone, wise.

In terms of the physical activities involved, there is an interesting
contrast between Hatha Yoga and lifting weights. Whereas the emphasis
in the former is on the **extension of the muscle,** to increase flexibility, in
the latter the focus is on the **contraction of the muscle** to increase size
and contractile strength. In Hatha Yoga, one stretches; in lifting
weights, one contracts.

Hatha Yoga grows from a Hindu culture. The philosophy underlying
the practice of the various yogas is one of Hinduism and Buddhism. In
contrast, weightlifting is not explicitly tied to a philosophical system, religious or secular. The implicit underlying philosophy which can be un-
covered if we dig a bit is one of pragmatism. Pragmatism is that no frills
American philosophy of "what works, works." "If it works, it's true." If
you do curls and your biceps get bigger, then curls work. This is a philosophy of practicality. To this we can add a bit of the "Protestant Ethic."
There is among most weightlifters that underlying belief that "hard work

is good," and "hard work brings rewards." Without waxing too philo-sophical, we can say that the implicit philosophy underlying most lifters' weightlifting activity is one of a practical work ethic. And this is, of course, a major philosophical stance in North America and much of Europe.

Earlier in the present chapter I stated that lifting weights is a path particularly suited to a Western world view. The statement of philo-sophical underpinnings, above, is one reason. Lifting weights has a very practical application in a society which values hard work and accom-plishment. Another factor, closely related to this, is that lifting weights is in the realm of what is tough, active, hard, forceful, effortful, willful, "masculine." These qualities are of service to the work ethic. And, they are another contrast with Hatha Yoga. Hatha Yoga is more in the realm of the tender, passive, soft, non-forceful, effortless, non-willful, "feminine." This contrast is valid in a very general sense. I intend no value judgment in this contrast. Neither is good or bad, in and of itself, or better or worse. In Taoist philosophy there are terms for these two realms which I have described. They are the Yang and the Yin, respec-tively. Yang is the force which causes contraction; Yin is the force which causes expansion. I recognize that **lifting weights is a strongly Yang activity,** whereas Hatha Yoga is a more Yin activity. So, in terms of paths, lifting weights is more suited for one for whom a Yang path has heart. Hatha Yoga is more suited for one for whom a Yin path has heart.

Clearly, I see an analogy between Hatha Yoga and lifting weights, or more specifically, bodybuilding, as a path. I believe that lifting weights is the Hatha Yoga of the West.

One of the ways that lifting weights can be instructive is by viewing the sports activity as representative of one's way of being-in-the-world. In other words, the lifting platform or the posing dais can be seen as a microcosm, reflecting how one is in her or his macrocosm or world as a whole. At times one's life seems so complex that it is difficult to gain self-perspective. This is the value of having a microcosmic view. Through the condensation and simplification offered by the microcosm one can gain self-knowledge. This, of course, requires self-attention, awareness and honesty. It requires that one observe one's self with care, concentra-tion, and lack of defensiveness.

Let us look at some of the dimensions of self-revelation which are likely in the weightlifting microcosm. Notice your mood while working out. Are you very serious or more playful? Easily distracted or very fo-cused on the exercise? Do you tend to be strict in the performance of the exercise or do you cheat? Are you hopeful and optimistic or pessimistic and resigned about the results? Do you give up easily when the lifting gets hard, or do you push through? Do you pace yourself so that you finish a workout with energy to spare or are you at the point of collapse? Do you plan a routine and stick to it, or do you play each workout by ear? Do you get bored with a particular exercise or routine easily, or do you stay with the same program for long periods of time? Are you experimental, trying out new routines, or do you prefer that with which you are familiar? Do you work out better alone, or in the presence of others, or with a training partner? When you look in the mirror do you look for progress to praise, or do you look for weaknesses about which to be critical? On the dais are you inflated with false confidence, supported by genuine confidence, or shy? On the lifting platform do you risk lifts at which you may fail, or do you open with a certain lift and make cautious increases, staying within the limits of fairly certain lifts?

The list of such questions is almost endless, being limited only by one's creativity and the level of honesty of one's self-reflection. The answers to these questions reveal and flesh out how one goes about the path of lifting weights. Personality is revealed in the "how" or "style" of behavior more than in the "what" or content of behavior. So, in the weightlifting microcosm one reveals her or his personal style by **how** he or she goes about lifting. Personal style tends to be fairly consistent over situations, so we can infer that how one is in the weightlifting microcosm, one is in her or his larger world. The point is that one's way or style of being-in-the-world is clear and easily observable in the microcosm of lifting weights.

I shall share a couple of examples from my own life. Although I have had workout partners, and from time to time invite someone to go work out with me, most of my weight training has been solo. In fact, much of my training, by choice, has been in my home gym. I have little difficulty getting myself started on a workout, and I am well self-sustained in my motivation to lift. These qualities of being self-motivated, self-sustained, and part of the time a loner are qualities that I exhibit in other arenas of my life as well. I have come to know these qualities as characteristic of how I live my life in general. But, it has been in the microcosm of lifting weights that I have had the most obvious encounter of these qualities in myself. In this microcosm I have become familiar with this personal style. In addition to this increased self-knowledge, I have at times struggled in my weightlifting microcosm with loneliness, highlighted by periods of training alone. I believe that my training alone has been of great help in my confronting my loneliness and has been an important part of my partial resolution of that painful theme in my life. This is but one example of how the weightlifting microcosm can be of value both in self-revelation and in resolution of conflicted areas in one's personality.

Another example is my low threshold for boredom. I like a lot of variety in my life, and from time to time get feedback from friends that they are amazed at how many things I am involved in and in how many areas I am accomplished. Again, this is clearly reflected in my weightlifting microcosm. I have done organizational/administrative work for the AAU, coached a YMCA Olympic lifting team, instructed body-building, have given public demonstrations of Olympic lifting and the proper exercise use of weights, have judged bodybuilding and Olympic lifting contests, and have done bodybuilding, powerlifting, and Olympic lifting, competing in the last, as well as in curling contests. I learned in this microcosm that in order to keep from getting bored and quitting, I could introduce variety, variations on the weightlifting theme. I learned to keep a balanced middle ground between boredom and dilitantism. (The dilitante moves from one thing to another so quickly that he or she doesn't have time to go to any depth with anything, thereby missing the benefits of each thing tried.) I learned to recognize the subtle clues in myself of when it was time for me to change exercise routine or even the activity. This knowledge of keeping to a middle ground between boredom and dilitantism, and the sensitivity to my own needs has translated well into my life as a whole.

One more example is something I learned in weightlifting competition itself. Lifting in competition has always been highly anxiety provoking for me. In every contest I have had that moment of questioning my wisdom in being there. Very early in my competitive experience I had a talk with myself, like an understanding coach or parent might do. I told myself that I was safe, there really was nothing to be afraid of, and to go ahead and do my best, and have fun. I have found that I have had the opportunity to go through this supportive pep talk before every competition. In this microcosm I discovered a process which I have extended to all spheres of my life. Years later, in my psychotherapy training, I learned about the technique of internal dialogue for dealing with disruptive emotional states. I learned in studying Transactional Analysis about giving support and protection to one's scared "Child ego state" from one's nurturing "Parent ego state." (I will discuss the process of internal dialogue in detail in Part II.) Once again, I made a discovery in my weightlifting microcosm which had application in the macrocosm of my life.

The idea is that by focusing one's awareness on one's self in the arena of lifting weights, one may greatly increase self-understanding and find means for coming to terms with personal issues in one's life.

There are some interesting parallels between lifting weights, particularly bodybuilding, and humanistic or growth oriented psychotherapy. Both psychotherapy and bodybuilding are systems for bringing about change in the person. In either case a short period of time may be spent to bring about some change, or a much longer period of time for more basic and dramatic change. The aim is to bring out the person's potential, to make that potential real. As such, both systems focus on aspects of what in humanistic psychology is termed "self-actualization." For psychotherapy the focus is on actualizing one's psychological (emotional, mental, spiritual) potential and for bodybuilding the primary focus is on actualizing one's physical (muscular) potential.

There is a paradox in self-actualization work which can be seen in bodybuilding and in psychotherapy. The paradox is that growth comes through accepting one's self, not through trying to make one's self different. That may sound strange, but bear with me. I am who and what I am. My nature is as it is and cannot be changed. So, trying to be different from what I am is an endeavor doomed to failure. If I try to be different I will be frustrating myself, and will most likely meet with resistance to the activity itself. To accept myself is to love myself, and not to accept myself is not to love myself. Part of my nature as a human being is to evolve and grow toward my potential. Therefore, if I accept who I am, love myself as I am, and nurture myself as I am, I will become more of what it is possible for me to be. Let me use an absurd example. Think of a baby antelope and a baby elephant. If the antelope rejects its nature and decides to develop the brute strength of an elephant, or the elephant rejects its nature and decides to grow up to be as fast and graceful as the antelope and to jump as high, both animals will live lives of abject frustration and defeat. They also will grow increasingly alienated from their genuine nature. Neither beast is more noble than the other. Both have a potential for great beauty when self-actualized.

In my psychotherapy practice I work with many people who are like the antelope trying to become an elephant, or the elephant trying to become an antelope. Their therapy task is to accept their true nature, give up their unrealistic dreams and illusions, and get about the business of developing their genuine selves.

In the arena of bodybuilding there are many antelopes trying to become elephants, and with much less frequency elephants trying to become antelopes. Since the contrast of individual differences is not as great among men or among women as it is across animal species such as antelopes and elephants, it is easier to deny their reality. So, many body-builders create an image of what they want to become based on the pictures of their idols in magazines or a viewing of their idols in a posing exhibition or contest. They then set out to actualize that image rather than to actualize their true potential. If it happens that their genetic potential is as great as that of their idol, then this process will probably work fairly well. Even so, at some point they will have to come to terms with the inevitability that they will never be exactly like the image which they are trying to actualize. For the majority of bodybuilders, however, their genetic potential is less than that of the idols from which they create their ideal image.

Most bodybuilders, I believe, are engaged in an attempt at "self-image actualization." They have fallen in love with an image, rather than having a healthy love for themselves. It is only through self-acceptance which comes from genuine self love that self-actualization can be approached. So, I am identifying two related dimensions each of which can be seen as a continuum: (1) self-actualization and self-image actualization; (2) self-actualization and non-actualization of the self (see Figure 2). These dimensions can be used for doing some soul searching. Where do you see yourself on each dimension? I believe strongly that the poles of self-image actualization and non-actualization of self are

Figure 2

Self-Actualization

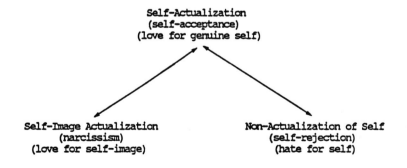

Self-Actualization
(self-acceptance)
(love for genuine self)

Self-Image Actualization
(narcissism)
(love for self-image)

Non-Actualization of Self
(self-rejection)
(hate for self)

negative. Being near these poles means inevitable unhappiness and lack of realization of one's true capacity for living. **Maximum personal growth is found neither through self-rejection nor narcissism, but through loving self-acceptance.** Put simply, this means for the body-builder neither to be hateful and rejecting of any part of her or his anatomy, nor to strive for an ideal image that is unrealistic and beyond her or his potential. So, if you have not inherited the potential for big calves, accept what you have as you, and seek to develop them to their potential. Your personal growth lies in your acceptance of what is, and in your developing to your God-given limits. Your personal growth does not lie in your being the biggest or the best. As an aside, I remember over-hearing Ray Mentzer say, just after being awarded the Mr. America trophy, that his father had bigger calves than he, and had never done a calf raise in his life! Remember, there is only one Arnold, or Lou, or Chris, or Sergio, or Frank, or Lee, or.... They are all different, and all beautiful. And there is only one you. And so are you.

Before leaving the psychotherapy-bodybuilding analogy, I want to cover three more things. First is the phenomenon of the "growing edge." In any arena of growth we can identify and think in terms of the next step in the process, the step which takes the person beyond where he or she has gone. This is the growing edge, the limit which the person is working to extend. In psychotherapy the therapeutic work is at the growing edge, facilitating the person in stepping beyond the previous limit into the territory of more nearly self-actualized living. In body-building the growing edge is, of course, the boundary between what one has attained physically, and the as yet not realized territory of physical realization.

There are several principles which characterize the growing edge phenomenon. Although these principles hold true for the growing edge of any realm or endeavor, I will illustrate them with an example that is easy to relate to for any veteran lifter. Let us use a limit lift as our example. Let us say that a particular lifter can bench press X pounds. His growing edge is the boundary between his personal best, X pounds, and the realm of what he is potentially capable of lifting. He will grow in his bench press as he gradually adds weight to his lift. I emphasize the grad-ual addition of weight. The "over-load principle" in weightlifting is that the body overcompensates for a particular lifting stress by muscular growth. So, rather than simply becoming accustomed to a particular lift, the body grows from that lift to the point of being able to do that plus a little more. The over-load principle dictates that increases in strength develop in small increments. So, our lifter will extend his growing edge by lifting $X + Y$ pounds, where X was his previous best, and Y is a small enough increment to allow success. (I do not want to complicate the example by getting into some of the advanced strategies such as partial lifts, assisted negative movements, and "cheating" exercises.)

If our lifter does not push his growing edge by "overloading" his muscles, his lift will not increase. In this case he is working too far behind his growing edge. Some of the research suggests that strength growth is most rapid from doing three sets of four to six repetitions with 80 to 90 percent of one's maximum. Lifters also know the importance of doing the maximum, or "maxing out" periodically. This means that lifting with less than $.8X$ will not lead to extension of the growing edge of our lifter's bench press.

Very early in my lifting career, I read a research article in *Science Digest* which claimed that maximum strength increase in a lift would result from warming up each day and then doing one rep with one's current maximum. I experimented with my Olympic press and indeed showed very nice progress for a week. After seven days my steady progress stopped, and I felt very bored with this regimen. Applying this to our lifter, it would be that he would warm up and then do a maximum bench press each day. He would bench press X or $X +$ every workout. Although this may work for a short period of time to stimulate a growth spurt, or to get over a sticking point in one's growing edge, it does not work as a regular routine. Too much time spent at one's growing edge, without respite, results in arrest of progress and a feeling of going stale. There is a stagnation. Physiologically there is not sufficient time for tissues to grow in response to such frequent overload, and psychologically there is not enough recovery time to allow for such frequent all out efforts.

The growing edge is a boundary to be played with, with a rhythm of pushing it, then backing off to that 80 to 90 percent range. If forced, by trying to take too large a step there may well be a backlash so that previous gains are lost. The growing edge may recede rather than progress. If the lifter in our example tries to make too large a jump in his poundage, he will fail at the lift, at least. Worse, he may injure himself. So, if he tries $X + Y +$ pounds, rather than $X + Y$, he may tear a pectoral muscle, injure a rotator cuff, or incur some other injury. I remember at a Southeastern United States Open bench press contest being struck with how many surgically scarred shoulders I saw. These telltale scars, marks of the surgeon, were evidence of attempts to force the growing edge. The setbacks from injury may be slight, or great. Several years ago I tore my left rotator cuff bench pressing. My choice was surgery or a long healing period. I opted for the latter and had to give up bench pressing completely for over a year. That was a dramatic recession of my growing edge in the bench press!

The growing edge does not progress constantly, but also regresses as it evolves. In other words, the growing edge evolves by going two steps forward and one back, two forward, one back. So, progress at the growing edge is not linear. If the lifter in our example were to make a graph of his bench press, with maximum lift on the vertical axis and time on the horizontal axis, the growth line would look like an inverted saw. Imagine a carpenter's hand saw turned blade up with the handle end on your right. The over-all trend is upward. But, within any short segment along the blade, there are ups and downs. This is the nature of the growing edge. Our lifter, on successive maximum lift days, may bench press X, X + 5 lb., X + 10 lb., X + 5 lb., X + 10 lb., X + 15 lb., X + 10 lb., etc.. The magnitude of increases and decreases will probably not be regular, but there will be a mix of progressions and regressions. These regressions result from the simple fact that our lifter can not always be at his best. There are too many factors which must all be optimal for being at his best — sleep, nutrition, mental stress, freedom from injury, enthusiasm, and so forth. An understanding of the fact that progress at the growing edge is not linear can save a lifter a great deal of frustration and discouragement. I see a failure to appreciate this fact in many training articles. They sometimes present the totally unrealistic goal of adding weight or repetitions every workout. A well-known Mr. America has even advised an increased pump of 1/16 to 1/8 inch every workout! This is a set up for failure.

The world of weights is an ideal microcosm for exploring the growing edge phenomenon. Here, one can experience the phenomenon with all of its sub-phenomena, and learn about one's way of relating to these. Since it applies to all areas of growth one can learn a great deal about how one relates to the issue of growth, regardless of what the content of that growth is. Figure 3 summarizes the major principles of the growing edge phenomenon.

Another analogy between lifting weights and psychotherapy which I want to share involves a particular therapeutic technique known as desensitization. Desensitization is frequently used in the treatment of phobias. Although there are variations in the method, in its basic form the patient is brought closer and closer to the feared object or situation, getting comfortable with each step before taking the next. By starting far

Figure 3

<u>**The Growing Edge Phenomenon**</u>

Principle 1:   The growing edge is at the boundary
                 between that which is actual
                 (accomplished) and that which is
                 potential (not yet accomplished).

Principle 2:   Growth occurs by extending the edge
                 gradually (in small increments) into the
                 range of the potential or possible.

Principle 3:   Working too far behind the growing edge
                 results in a lack of growth.

Principle 4:   Spending too much time working at the
                 growing edge without respite results in
                 stagnation (arrest of progress).

Principle 5:   Forcing beyond the growing edge (taking
                 too large increments) results in a
                 backlash (loss of previous growth).

Principle 6:   Progress at the growing edge is
                 non-linear (the "inverted saw").

enough away from the feared object or situation and by moving toward it in small enough increments, the phobic person is eventually able to come in contact with that object or situation without ever becoming anxious. In this way the person is "de-sensitized." Here is an example. Let us say we have a man who is acrophobic. A therapist might desensitize this man by taking him to a stadium with open bleachers. He would have the man take as many steps up the bleachers as possible without feeling anxiety. That could mean just looking at the bleachers, or it could mean taking several steps up. The man would go slowly, looking up and down after taking each step, and repeating this same procedure until absolutely comfortable. Then he would take one more step up, and so on, until at some time he could go all the way to the top, look down, and remain relatively comfortable. Depending on the patient's goals, he and the therapist could extend this procedure to other situations involving heights—open hotel balconies, glass elevators, mountain lookouts, and so forth. This desensitization procedure could take a few days, a few weeks, or many months, depending on their rate of work, the severity of the phobia, and the patient's ultimate goal. The principles of the growing edge phenomenon, of course, are applicable here.

There is a clear analogy between desensitization and lifting weights. The analogy becomes clearer when we use the phrase "progressive resistance exercise." In both cases there is a goal, and the method is to "sneak up on it" gradually enough that one succeeds with each progressive step. In classic analogy form —

Desensitization:Phobia::Progressive resistance exercise:Weightlifting goal

Whether it is one more step up the bleachers or five more pounds on the bar, the principle is the same.

The final analogy between lifting weights and psychotherapy which I want to draw concerns pain and the fear of pain. Psychological growth often involves emotional pain. It involves the sometimes painful process of acknowledging what one would rather avoid, and struggling with that until one reaches some degree of resolution. It is that willingness to confront and to sustain that confrontation which allows for the resolution and personal growth. Many times people avoid the confrontation out of fear of the attendant pain, and thereby rob themselves of the opportunity for growth. So each time one bumps up against an issue which defines her or his growing edge, there is a choice to be made. The person can either stay comfortable by avoiding or can engage in a growthful way, enduring the pain. The decision is between the "growth choice" and the "fear choice." So, it is the fear of emotional pain, or "pain phobia" which is the enemy of growth.

Turning to lifting, the issue is similar. The popular phrase is, "No pain, no gain." Any veteran of the weight sports is familiar with physical pain — the burning deep in the belly of a muscle during a hard set, the aching of a well-worked muscle hours or even days later. These are the growth pains with which any serious lifter must come to terms. Any lifter who shies away from such pain is going to rob herself or himself of most of the growth that is possible. How many would-be lifters have gotten scared of the pain, or out of an intolerance for discomfort have given up the sport? I also wonder how many lifters reduce their workouts to a mere act of going through the motions without benefiting in gains because of holding themselves back from the pain zone. Again, as in psychotherapy, the pain phobia is the enemy of growth. Those who maximize their growth potential, whether in the realm of psychotherapy or the realm of the lifting sports, are those who are committed enough to growth-oriented experiencing that they are willing to endure a reasonable degree of pain. They are free from the pain phobia. (I will discuss pain further in a later chapter.)

Another area of personal growth for which the weightlifting path is well suited is that of body awareness. Both the activity of lifting and the results of lifting are sources of information about one's embodied self. So, by reflecting on one's experience in lifting and by carefully observing the immediate and later results of one's lifting, much can be learned. By increasing one's body awareness, one becomes more informed and attuned, thus opposing the forces which push toward body alienation.

Body awareness is served through three sources of information. First is internal sensation. Second is touching one's body. Third is seeing one's body. Let us examine each of these in turn.

Perhaps the first glint of enhanced body awareness experienced by the beginning lifter comes from the internal sensations while lifting. As one performs a new exercise the internal sensations inform as to what body parts and sub parts are called into action. So one learns from feeling the pull and the mechanical stress what muscles produce what movements. This is not the learning of Latin names for muscles depicted by drawings of figures denuded of skin, but an experiential lesson in personal gross anatomy and biomechanics. Next time you lift, attend to the internal sensations. Feel what is taking place inside as you curl the weight. As you concentrate on those sensations you may discover what part of your biceps strains at the beginning, where the strain shifts throughout the range of motion of the exercise, and where the origin and insertion of your biceps are. Continued close observation may reveal the location of the muscles which assist the prime mover biceps. And even more subtle is the message of the stabilizing muscles which hold one's body in position such that the prime mover and its synergists are able to enact the curl.

If this stress sensation is a whisper to be listened for, the burning sensation in the muscle is a shout which cannot erupt without notice. So, as one lifts, the burn is like a swelling voice from the muscle demanding credit for doing the work. As one curls, the increasing burn leaves no mistake as to what muscle is the prime mover. The burning biceps demands attention as the main activator in the curl. In the case of some exercises the voice of stress in the muscles is difficult to localize with precision. It is in these cases that the undeniable shout of the burn is particularly important for one's growth in awareness.

A third internal sensation which informs the lifter is the muscle soreness which develops several hours after the workout. Whereas the sensations of muscle stress and muscle burn are immediately available to the lifter as he or she lifts, the sensation of soreness is delayed, arriving some considerable time after the lifting is over. Some of its information is redundant. For example, the sore biceps a day or two after doing curls only calls attention again to the fact that the biceps were the prime movers. This fact would already have been apparent from the burning during the execution of the curls, if not from the biceps stress as well. But, sometimes there is new information in the delayed muscle soreness. With some exercises the stress seems so diffuse, involving so many muscles, that there is no easily identifiable prime mover. And, sometimes an exercise does not produce a burn. In these cases, it is the delayed soreness which is most informative. I offer an example from when I first used chin-ups as an exercise. When I performed the chinning movement I would feel the stress in my biceps, primarily. If I did enough repetitions, I would get a strong burn in my biceps. But, to my surprise, the soreness the next day was in my lats! The delayed soreness gave me information about myself which wasn't offered through the more immediate feedback of stress and muscle burn.

I have come to anticipate muscle soreness with appreciation and excitement. The feedback which soreness gives me tells me two things. First it tells me what muscles I worked hard, and second it tells me that I was working at my growing edge. Both of these revelations are of value, and are used by top lifters. For instance, I remember hearing Bill Pearl say in a seminar that "Something must hurt all the time, if you are a bodybuilder." It is this soreness that gives evidence of working at the growing edge.

Muscle soreness is a self communication, a way of giving one's self information. From this feedback I have learned what muscles are involved in a particular exercise, as in my example, above. When I hear or read of an exercise which is new to me and want to try it, I use my consequent soreness as a major source of information in my evaluation of the exercise. So if I try a new triceps exercise, but develop soreness in my shoulders, I reject that exercise (as a triceps exercise). Arnold Schwarzenegger (1977) has written about using this soreness as a guide for determining "what exercise does what" for one's self.

Muscle soreness, if attended to, can be an excellent teacher of one's own anatomy. Many times I had looked at anatomy charts and seen the location of the soleus. But translating such a drawing to my body was difficult, and my soleus remained a vague abstraction located underneath my gastrocnemius. One day I worked out in a gym which had a seated calf machine. Fascinated with the novelty of this new toy, I did several heavy sets. The next day I **was** soleus muscles more than anything else. It was as if my embodiment were in my soleus muscles. Out of vague background, my soleus muscles emerged as a persistent figure in my internal perception. I now know exactly where they are and what their function is.

If muscle stress is the whisper of the body's inner message, and muscle burn is the sudden shout, muscle soreness is the delayed, but persistent talk. These three voices from within are valuable informants in the quest for expanded body awareness.

A second source of information about one's body and the effects of lifting is touch. One can touch one's self after an exercise and feel how turgid the affected muscles are. Touching in this way reveals the degree of pump as reflected both in size and hardness. Though more subtle to the touch, one can also feel a heated area after an exercise. Again, this "hot spot" informs the lifter as to what body part has been worked most. Just as the burn is experienced internally, the sensation of heat can be felt when the skin surface is touched immediately after the exercise.

I mentioned earlier that there are three sources which can serve to enhance body awareness. The third is seeing. For many people there is a taboo against looking carefully and really seeing. For them the implicit rule is "glance, but don't see." If one is to use seeing as a path to body awareness and an escape from body alienation this taboo must be overcome. There are at least three worthwhile things to look for. One is the change in skin color following an exercise. I enjoy standing close to a mirror and looking at my shoulders and upper arms following a shoulder or upper arm exercise. I look for the bluish net-like pattern which has spread over some portion of my shoulders and upper arms. I know this to be an indication of engorgement; my veins (which are closer to the surface than arteries) and venioles are full of deoxygenated (bluish) blood.

The lifter can also look at herself or himself in the mirror to see her or his pump. This is the primary purpose of the mirrors lining the walls of a bodybuilding gym. The mirrors are there for looking at one's self, to see the pump that develops during the course of a workout. By carefully observing the pump, one can learn what exercises, repetitions, and sets are optimal for its development in one's self.

The mirror is useful in observing one's self over time, as well. This time spent looking carefully at one's self is a way of getting and staying

acquainted with one's body. This intimate knowing counteracts ignorance of one's self, if not self-alienation. Figure 4 summarizes the guides
to body awareness through lifting. (I have not included the use of the
tape measure, since this is not so much a tool for enhancing body awareness as it is a quantification and objectification of self-touching.)

In the succeeding chapters of Part I I will explore some specific issues
which arise in the course of traversing the path of lifting weights. For
now, let us consider lifting weights as a path of enlightenment through
experience in the flesh. Let us see it as a path to harmony, clarity, and
calm. This can be realized as one lifts with an attitude of self-respect, cu-
riosity, and exquisite awareness.

Figure 4

Body Awareness through Lifting

	Immediate Feedback (During an exercise) (Activity based)	Short Delay in Feedback (During a workout) (Results based)	Delayed Feedback (Hours or more after a workout) (Results based)
Internal Sensations	Muscle stress Muscle burn		Muscle soreness
Touching		Pump Heat on skin	Muscle hypertrophy
Seeing		Pump Change in skin color	Muscle hypertrophy

Chapter 3

WHY WE LIFT:
THE DEEPER MOTIVES

IN CHAPTER 1 I identified four motives for lifting weights. I named these motives "I Should," "I Have to," "I Want to," and the "Path for Personal Growth." Important as these distinctions of motive are, they are not sufficient to fully understand why people devotedly lift weights. These four motives are relatively easily recognized, or, we might say, are surface motives. If we look more deeply, however, we find motives which ·may be unconscious and thus operate for the most part outside the lifter's awareness.

Lifting weights is usually an overdetermined behavior, I believe. Just as I suggested in Chapter 1 that more than one of those surface motives may be operating at the same time with a particular lifter, more than one of the deeper motives to be discussed in the present chapter may be operating coincidentally. It is to these deeper or more inferred motives that I now want to attend.

In order to understand unconscious motivation to lift weights, we need first to understand the peculiar challenges of the lifting sports. Just what does lifting weights uniquely offer? There are several basic parameters of exercise: strength, speed, flexibility, endurance, and coordination. These are the components of physical activity, itself. Although these parameters may seem self-explanatory, I believe some brief explanations would be helpful to our understanding here. In reversed order, coordination means the timing of movement. It means putting several movements in a particular sequence and with a particular rhythm such that a particular effect is produced. Endurance refers to the ability to continue an activity through time. It includes both muscular endurance and respiro-circulatory endurance. Flexibility is a measure of

35

the range of motion of body parts, or the extent of their excursion as they are moved to their limits. The rate at which one is able to perform a particular movement is referred to as speed. And, finally, strength is a measure of the amount of resistance which one can overcome in the execution of a movement. With these five dimensions in mind one can evaluate any given physical movement or activity. On a grosser level, a particular sport can be analyzed in terms of these parameters. Any given sport has its own peculiar profile, requiring more or less development of each of these five dimensions. To do well in any physical activity requires a certain level of development of all of these, but certain activities are outstanding in their demands in terms of certain dimensions. We can think of particular sports or physical disciplines which are extreme in the focused demand on a particular parameter of movement. Some such pairings which I think of are coordination and figure skating, endurance and the triathlon, flexibility and Hatha Yoga, speed and sprinting, strength and powerlifting. (Incidentally, the name "powerlifting" is a bit of a misnomer. Technically, "power" is a measure of "work" peformed per unit of time. "Work," in turn is defined in physics as "force times distance." So, for example, 1 "horsepower" is equal to 550 lb. lifted 1 foot in 1 second. A deadlifter who picks up a 550 lb. barbell 1 foot in 1 second has generated 1 horsepower. His competitor who lifts 560 lb., 1 foot, but takes 3 seconds to do so, has generated far less power but is declared the winner. Powerlifting is, more accurately, "brute-strength lifting.")

Although the degree of involvement of coordination, endurance, flexibility, and speed differ among the weight sports, what they hold in common is an extreme emphasis on development and demonstration of strength (in bodybuilding, the emphasis is on the development of muscular hypertrophy which reflects and symbolizes strength, even though the strength is not demonstrated directly). If strength is valued highly, then the weight sports will have high appeal. So far, however, we have not tapped the deeper psychological level. To do so, I enlist the notion of the "archetype" as developed by Carl Jung.

Jung (1968) hypothesized that, in addition to the personal unconscious so thoroughly explored by Freud, there exists a "collective unconscious." This deeper unconscious manifests itself through universal images expressed in dreams, religious beliefs, myths, and fairy tales. Jung referred to the structural components of the collective unconscious by several names, one of which was "archetype." The archetypes derive from the accumulated experience of humankind and are inherited just as the form of the nervous system is inherited. Archetypes then function as universal thought forms, serving as a frame of reference with which to experience the world. Examples are god (good), devil (evil), earth mother, hero, unity, magic, birth, death, rebirth, old wise man, male principle, female principle, and self.

The archetype, as a universal thought form, does not have a predetermined content, but is a possibility of representation which can be actualized in any number of ways. Jung demonstrated through his research that archetypes are not only passed down through tradition and language (myth, religion, folklore), but can arise spontaneously, as in dreams and art. Archetypes can combine, and so, for example, the primordial images of wise old man and hero can interfuse to produce the conception of the "philosopher king."

Allow me one example of how an archetype can become manifest. The child inherits a readiness or tendency to have certain experiences. By virtue of the human nervous system, as it has evolved to this point in time, the child is programmed to recognize certain universal motifs. This is shared by all humans, by virtue of the human nervous system, or in psychological terms, the collective unconscious. The child's archetype of mother produces a primordial image of mother, and through this the child can "recognize" mothering as it is presented through the person of a literal mother. The child's preformed conception of "mother" then determines in part how the child perceives her or his actual mother. The child's experience of her or his mother will be, then, a combination and interaction of the mother archetype (universal inner disposition) and the actual behavior of its mother (specific, literal events).

With this basic understanding of archetypes, we can return to the question of the deep psychological appeal of lifting weights. One of the primordial images recognized by Jung is the archetype of strength or power. The strength or power archetype is a predisposition to perceive and to be fascinated by power. It leads to a desire to create and control power. When an archetype is tapped into, there is often a rather mystical quality to one's experience. Perhaps you can recognize in yourself that mystical fascination in some experience with an event of power. Some examples of situations which would elicit or invite such archetypal experience with power are fireworks displays, drag racing, pile drivers, a heavy surf, a tractor pull, a violent storm, and firing a high-powered gun. Recall when you have been mesmerized by such an event, or have observed someone else so entranced by such an occurrence. I remember, vividly, standing on the rim of Mauna Loa while the volcano was active, enraptured as time stood still. I was completely in awe of the incomprehensible power as I felt the intense heat of the rising air currents, smelled the sulphur fumes, and watched the molten lava bubble and flow.

But, again, I have mentioned lifting weights only to go on about the power archetype in general. In the above examples of experiences with power I mentioned natural events and two categories of man-made events, machinery and chemical explosions. The events which are focal to our discussion, however, are the events in which men or women perform an act of strength, thereby tapping into the archetype of power. What I am proposing is that **the weight sports are valued insofar as they provide a primitive, personally-embodied manifestation of the power archetype.** That is, **the act of lifting weights is a living out through one's own body the archetype of strength.** A special intimacy with the power archetype is afforded insofar as it is given life through an event of one's body rather than being observed outside one's self, controlled (as in the case of operating machinery or setting off an explosion) or not controlled (as in natural events).

I have come to believe that **it is this embodied living-out-into-the-world of the strength archetype which is the primary (i.e., deepest, most primitive, most basic) motivation for lifting weights.** All other motivations, valid as they are, are secondary. To recognize power and to want to control it is an orientation we derive from the collective unconscious. The most direct way of controlling it is to manifest it through one's body, to be strong, to **be** strength. When one performs an act of strength, there is a congruence between what is manifested and the unconscious archetypal pattern. This congruence is experienced in various degrees as interest, fascination, or awe. An eternal and universal truth is known.

Jung emphasized the universal expression of the archetypes in myth, folklore, religion, visions, art and dreams. There are obvious examples of the strength archetype manifesting across cultures. Looking at Western civilization, we can find a plethora of examples from our earliest written records to the present. In I Samuel, Chapter 4, verse 9 it is written, "Be strong, and quit yourselves like men...." Often we find a blending of the strength archetype with the hero archetype. In Greek mythology we find Atlas, the leader of the Titans in their contest with Zeus, who for eternity bears the heavens on his head and hands. The great hero of the Greeks, known for his strength and endurance, was, of course, Herakles (Latinized as Hercules). The Old Testament presents us with Samson and his incredible feats of strength, performed when his faith pleased his god. Beowulf was the strong hero in the West Saxon epic of about 700 A.D.. Such heroes of strength continue today as the Saturday morning cartoon "superheroes" dash upon the screen with grossly hypertrophied muscles. Conan, Superman, the Incredible Hulk; the list could be extended. The point is that the strength archetype, often interpenetrated with the hero archetype, is well represented in the world's literature, from its beginning until now.

It seems that of the weight sports it is bodybuilding which most clearly interfuses at least an element of the hero archetype with the strength archetype. The hero is recognized as such only after he has done something heroic. So, too, the bodybuilder is judged after he has done what he does, after he has trained. The names of the contests, and titles awarded also suggest the conferring of hero status on the winner. Rarely, if ever, has a winning powerlifter or Olympic style lifter been given a "Mr.," "Miss," or "Ms." title. But consider how we designate a physique winner. Even the smallest local contest confers its "Mr. Prairie City" award. One of the first physique contests I attended was the "Mr. Hercules" contest, held the evening that Steve Reeves' movie made its debut in town. (That was three or four years before I attended the "Mr. Avon Beach" event.) The big physique events are clearly infused with an element of the hero archetype. Consider the titles of Mr., and where appropriate, the women's equivalent, U.S.A., America, World, Universe, and, if any question remains, Olympia.

If the hero archetype is less in manifest evidence in powerlifting and Olympic style weightlifting, the strength archetype is manifested in a form more raw. The physique contestant displays a body which suggests strength and stands as a symbol for it. The competitive lifter, on the other hand, demonstrates strength in its raw form.

Just as the physique contestant draws on the hero archetype to augment her or his living out a symbolic portrayal of the power archetype, the competitive lifter may draw, to some degree, on the archetype of magic. A heavy lift is clearly a demonstration of power. But it may also touch lightly on the realm of magic. A good lifter is able to lift a weight far in excess of what a nonlifter of comparable body weight could. Sometimes these feats seem almost beyond human ability. These are acts apparently in defiance of gravity. It appears as if the lifter is able to partially suspend, or at least reduce the ordinary gravitational pull, to alter the law of gravity. This is an appearance not only to the spectator, but may also be noted by the lifter herself or himself. As I write this I am recalling the sensation I had when as a teenage lifter I did an Olympic

press of 190 lb. at a bodyweight of 140 lb.. Somehow, it was almost as if
the weight were floating up. Paradoxical as it sounds, I felt at the same
time as if I were and were not pressing the weight. I have experienced
this many times while performing maximum or near maximum lifts.
This is not always the case with a maximum lift, however. Sometimes
the weight seems extremely heavy, and is lifted only with the greatest of
effort. When I was training for powerlifting competition, I was fascinated with the two different experiences which I regularly had in the
deadlift, sometimes the effortful lift, sometimes that "magical" floating
lift where I seemed as much the observer as the active lifter. When I began breaking the 400 lb. mark with regularity (at a bodyweight around
160 lb.) I discovered how to create the floating sensation in the lift.
What I discovered worked like "magic." (I will describe the procedure in
a later chapter on techniques to enhance lifting performance.) Levita-
tion of objects has long been a feat worthy of the best of the legendary
"magicians." A lifter can create such an illusion with the most astounded
and delighted witness being her or himself.

I am suggesting a corollary to my above stated belief about the power
archetype being at the root of weightlifting's attraction. **I believe that in
addition to tapping into the power archetype, as all forms of lifting
do, bodybuilding taps into the hero archetype and competitive lifting may at times tap into the archetype of magic.** The bodybuilder
lives out an embodied manifestation of the strength archetype interpenetrated with the hero archetype. The competitive lifter may be closer to
living out an embodied manifestation of the archetype of power, by itself. Some competitive lifters, at times, may also infuse their performance with the perspective of magic.

Each sport, each form of exercise, each physical activity presents its
own unique challenge. Lifting weights is the activity *par excellence* for encountering the power archetype. Lifting weights is a way of bringing
one's self face to face with all of the issues attending strength. Given that
the power archetype is a potential force and form in all of us, lifting
weights is a path for exploring and actualizing that potential. By lifting
weights we bring forth a natural part of us and give life to something
dormant. Developing and experiencing strength is an act, then, of self-
actualization. It is the realization of a potential core human experience.

Perhaps the most controversial topic in the iron world has been the advent of women bodybuilders. There have been "strongwomen" since the
days of vaudeville. But these women were, for the most part, regarded as
oddities, interesting as they were. In recent years, women have become a

large force in bodybuilding, Olympic lifting, and powerlifting. The fact of women in the two latter sports has been accepted pretty well as a more or less natural development. The acceptance of women in bodybuilding, in contrast, has been fraught with controversy and heated polemic. This degree of concern suggests some deep, psychological dynamic. I believe this state of affairs is understandable, again, with the aid of the theory of archetypes. Jung identified several archetypes which have evolved to such a high degree that they deserve to be viewed separately from the many other archetypes of the collective unconscious, and regarded, instead as distinct elements of the personality. Two of these, the "anima" and the "animus," represent the feminine and the masculine principles, respectively. Remember, the anima and the animus are archetypes, highly evolved, and as such are forms which serve as frames of reference for experience. The anima is the unconscious side of a man's conscious masculinity, and the animus is the unconscious side of a woman's femininity. For each, it is the respective unconscious archetype which allows an empathic understanding of the opposite sex.

The difficulty which many people have had with women in bodybuilding has been that they thought the women did not look feminine. They did not look soft and curvacious. And, so the schism in women's bodybuilding evolved. Some contests awarded their honors to the more "feminine" looking bathing beauty type, while other contests chose as winners those who looked lean, angular, hard, in a word, muscular. The tradition had been set by the Miss America and Miss Universe contests and their regional and local versions. These were contests for bathing beauties. Then along came the women with muscles. Clearly, muscles have traditionally been associated with masculinity. Note the similarity of the words "masculine" and "muscular." The stem words "mascul" and "muscul" differ by only one vowel. If that were not enough, we can be informed by the etymological fact that the Sanskrit root word for muscle is "muska," meaning "scrotum." And here we have the issue that for some is a problem. The issue is that women bodybuilders are displaying a high degree of development of something which is associated with the masculine — muscles. The problem is for people who insist on a simple world where black is black and white is white, or more to the point, men are masculine (muscular) and women are feminine (not muscular).

Jung insisted, as Freud had before him, that human beings are not so exclusively masculine or feminine as some people would have it. Rather than black or white, the human situation is black and white, and also some black within the white and some white within the black. This is profoundly symbolized by the Yin Yang symbol of Taoism. Jung's way of saying this is that the man carries the anima within him and the woman carries the animus within her. The development and expression of the anima or the animus aspect of one's person is a part of one's develop-ment of wholeness or self-realization.

For a woman, then, the task of self-actualization includes the realiza-tion of her animus. While her animus is denied and repressed, she is in-complete, she has not actualized an important aspect of her potential being. Lifting weights is a direct avenue to the primitive, archetypal level of experiencing the animus. I suggest that **women bodybuilders may be unconsciously motivated by the urge to live out and expe-rience their animus in the dramatic and blatant form of a highly muscled body.** As I see it, a woman bodybuilder is bringing forth an as-pect of her being which has not been welcome in our culture in such a stark and dramatic physical expression. Whether or not someone likes that muscular look is another question, a question of personal esthetic preference.

Just as lifting weights can bring forth the woman's animus, it is a way for the man to give emphasis to his masculinity. The psychology of Alfred Adler (Hall and Lindzey, 1970) is particularly useful in the understanding of the motivation for this. Adler observed that when someone has a physi-cal weakness, some underdeveloped or inferior body part, the person will tend to compensate by trying to develop that part through intensive train-ing. The classic examples are of Demosthenes, who, although a stutterer as a child, became a great orator, and Theodore Roosevelt who overcame his childhood puniness to become a strong, robust man. Adler's idea was that one's feeling of inferiority leads to an attempt at compensation. He termed this striving for compensation the "masculine protest." As he broadened his view over the years, he came to see that feelings of inferior-ity can arise from a sense of incompletion or imperfection in any sphere of life, and lead to compensatory behavior. Behind this compensatory be-havior is a "striving for superiority." Adler believed that "striving for supe-riority" is an innate urge, a natural part of life. It is this basic motivation which carries a person from one stage of development to the next, and keeps one wanting to grow throughout one's life. It is "the great upward drive," a striving for completion. As such, "striving for superiority" is parallel to Jung's concept of "self-realization," and the concept of "self-actualization" in humanistic psychology.

As a deep motive, then, a man's feeling of physical inferiority may lead him into a "striving for superiority" via the barbells. The more keenly felt the inferiority, and the more hopeful and optimistic about successfully compensating for that, the more devoted one may be in his pumping of iron. Remember, the key to understanding this motive is the subjective experience. What is important is the degree of self-perceived inferiority. A man may be small, weak, and even puny, relative to other men, but may or may not experience a feeling of inferiority. Likewise, a large, strong man may feel physically inferior despite objective evidence to the contrary. So it is when a man **feels** physically inferior regardless of the objective case, that he is likely to seek out a compensatory experience. Lifting weights, of course, is an obvious choice when it is available.

I think it is good to recognize this Adlerian "striving for superiority" as a deep motive for lifting weights without becoming moralistic and critical. My purpose here is not to judge this motive as good or bad, but to acknowledge it as a probable dynamic in many men's choice to lift weights.

This motive has seemed so obvious to me, since it sparked my beginnings with the weights. When I was a boy, my father tried to get me interested in lifting. He lifted regularly both at home and at a gym. Although I sometimes watched him work out, had access to a variety of equipment, and even knew the names of many exercises and what they were for, I felt no urge to participate. I was simply uninterested. I started high school young, still twelve when I walked through the door for the first time, and weighed 98 lb.. It was a couple more years before I started lifting. A girl friend and some teasing from the "jocks" led to my taking stock of my physical being, and a clear sense of inferiority. My feelings of physical inferiority sparked me to avail myself of all that iron in the garage, and I became a devout lifter. The mental shift was dramatic. I changed from being indifferent to lifting to truly loving it in a matter of weeks. I soon identified with weightlifting as "my sport," and felt a self-identification as a weightlifter. Without that feeling of inferiority, I doubt that I would ever have become a hardcore lifter.

As I touched upon, above, along with the feeling of inferiority, the hope for successful compensation by means of lifting is necessary or else one would not lift, but would seek out some other form of physical training. So, one may sally forth on the weight path sufficient with this faith and hope. Soon, however, hope will dim, if the hard work is not rewarded by some experience of successful compensation. A gain in weight, a new bulge where there had been only "skin and bone," a lift with five more pounds all provide early reinforcement. My first big reinforcement came less than two years after I started lifting, with my winning a state weightlifting title. That little plastic and metal trophy was the concrete evidence which symbolized that I had successfully compensated for my beginning state of inferiority. To have gone from weak and puny to a locally recognized winning athlete in less than two years felt to me like a huge reward. With this magnitude of reinforcement, of course I continued lifting.

What becomes of this "masculine protest" after the inferiority has been adequately compensated? Two things, I believe. First, as Adler described the "striving for superiority," there is no end. It is not just a move from "inferior" to "no longer inferior," but it is a life-long striving for completion and wholeness. It is, as I wrote a few paragraphs back, parallel to self-actualization and self-realization. As such, it is a driving force to carry one from one plateau to the next, perpetually. Second, the activity which was the means of successful compensation may then become an end in itself. What I am suggesting is that lifting weights, begun as a means to compensate for physical inferiority, may in time, come to be cherished for itself. The psychological term for this, as introduced by Gordon Allport (1961), is "functional autonomy." In the beginning one may lift with the hope of overcoming inferiority, later because of the success experienced, and still later, out of a love for lifting, *per se*. In this third stage the act of lifting has become functionally autonomous, no longer tied to either hope or the reinforcement of success. It is as if one lifts in this third stage to honor and be with the experience which once was so important in transporting one from the realm of inferiority. This is not merely habit, nor is it neurotic compulsion, but rather the pleasure of the company of an old friend.

A woman, too, may experience a sense of Adlerian inferiority. And, she may choose the animus oriented expression of "masculine protest" in her striving for superiority. An additional factor can be the woman's wish to prove herself in the "masculine" realm because of familial and societal messages which have denigrated the "feminine." It is no accident that the growth in women's bodybuilding, Olympic lifting, and power-lifting has been on the heels of the "women's movement." "Feminism" has led to greater recognition and expression of the animus by many women. Nowhere is this more blatant than in women's pumping of iron. Lifting weights offers a special opportunity, therefore, for a woman to claim her equality. The old phrase, "the weaker sex," is forcefully thrown out every time a woman steps onto a lifting platform and hefts a weight which untrained men in the audience, of comparable body weight, could not lift.

Lifting weights can be an avenue to what Abraham Maslow (1968) has identified as "peak experiences." These experiences give one's life a special sparkle, a special joy, a grounding in experienced profundity. Most everyone who has spent much time engaged in hardcore lifting recognizes peak experiences as something that just happens from time to time. A systematic investigation of peak experiences in sports was conducted by Kenneth Ravizza (1977) several years ago. Although he did not interview lifters in his study, he did include representatives from 12 different sports, both team and individual, at three levels of proficiency (recreational, university team, Olympic). His results showed that participation in sports often does lead to peak experiences. More specifically, when he asked the athletes to describe what characterized their "greatest moment" while participating in sports, the following emerged. Over half of the athletes reported an unusual richness of perception during the experience, a uniqueness of the event, and a fusion of the athlete with the event (so it was as if the event took over and the person were no longer doing it). Eighty percent or more of those interviewed revealed a transcendence of the ordinary self (they became so absorbed in the activity that it was as if there was a union with the phenomenon). Maslow has referred to this as an "ego-transcending experience," a sense of awe and wonder of the experience, and a disorientation in time and space. Ninety to ninety-five percent spoke of an effortless, passive perception, a perception of the universe as integrated and unified, a self-validating experience of the activity itself (winning or losing seemed of little importance), a feeling of being so in control as to feel almost godlike, a feeling that the experience was perfect, and a total immersion in the activity (giving full attention to the activity). Of Ravizza's sample, all spoke of a loss of fear during the activity. (Although other characterizations were given as well as these, the ones mentioned above coincide with qualities which Maslow discussed as occurring with peak experiences.) Surely, this is a spiritual experience, a glimpse through the window of ecstasy.

To be explicit, I am suggesting that in the overdetermination of the motivation to lift weights, the urge for peak experiences can figure, too. Another eternal truth is reached.

A few years ago, I served on the dissertation committee of a doctoral candidate in clinical psychology at Georgia State University, Robin Brill. In her study, as yet unpublished, she showed several central elements expressed by weightlifters concerning their experience of their sport. Common experiences included the sublimation of their frustration and aggression into the physical activity of lifting, self-discipline and singleness of purpose, pride in self (with body as referent), power of the mind to determine physical ability, and an increased confidence and feeling of superiority over others (with body as referent).

Staying for the moment with research findings, Larry Tucker (1982, 1983) has shown in his studies that there is an increase in global internal and external self concept in college males taking a weightlifting course.

The results of these research studies seem to be consistent with my proposed deeper motivations to lift weights. The studies generated data which are at a different level from the level at which these deeper motivations lie. However, there is a consistency between the two levels which can be inferred.

There is one final deep motivation which may operate with some lifters. That is the motivation of risk-taking. Some background is necessary before saying more about the risk in lifting weights. Sol Roy Rosenthal (Leonard, 1974, 1975) has stated that a certain amount of risk is a basic evolutionary need and is essential in our lives. He divides sports into two categories, RE (risk exercise) and non-RE, seeing the former as having the special importance of providing a good source of risk taking. Skiing and rock climbing are examples of RE sports, as contrasted with the non-RE sports, golf and tennis. Rosenthal believes that RE and non-RE sports have different effects on the participant. In addition, he states that the enjoyment of non-RE sports is often tied to winning, whereas the RE sports are more likely to be enjoyed for their own sake, with competition being of less importance. It is the tension between highly developed skill and calculated risk which creates the exhilaration of RE sports. Research conducted by Rosenthal suggested that participation in RE sports makes men and women more efficient at work, more creative, and more productive, as well as improving their sex lives.

Now, to relate this to the iron game. Certainly, lifting weights does not involve the dramatic risks found in skydiving, rock climbing, or downhill skiing. On the other hand, the risk of serious injury far exceeds such risk in golf, tennis, or volleyball. In bodybuilding the risk may be kept to a minimum. However, in Olympic style lifting and powerlifting the risk of serious injury is frequently present. On limits days and in competition the lifter is pushing a limit beyond where he or she has been before, and in so doing risks serious injury either from a strained body or a body crushed by a dropped weight.

As I am writing, I am remembering watching a powerlifter in a meet. As he squatted, one of his ankles gave way, turning under, and he fell. He was saved from possibly being crushed by several hundred pounds of falling iron, by two alert spotters. Another time I saw a man lose consciousness while straining to break the world Olympic press record. He fell backwards, flat on his back, to a loud clatter of iron plates.

I know that this element of risk has beckoned me back to heavy lifting several times after I have given it up. Some of my most vivid and exciting memories of lifting involve these dangerous situations. I recall falling forward, while attempting a squat, and feeling the bar roll over my neck and the back of my head as the ground rushed toward us. My two spotters stood motionless watching, as if in a trance. Another time, in competition, I lost control of the bar just before locking out on a jerk. The weight came down behind me, just grazing my upper back and tearing off some skin as the knurling of the Olympic bar dug in on its rapid descent to the platform.

What I am suggesting is that Olympic lifting and powerlifting, where exceedingly heavy weights are moved about, over one's body (except in the case of the deadlift), are, to a degree, risk-exercise sports. To the degree that one engages in these, then one may be motivated by the exhilaration attendant with the inherent risk.

To understand why we lift weights requires that we admit of overdetermination. It requires that we understand the coexistence of both conscious and unconscious motivations. And, finally, it requires an appreciation of such forces as risk taking, peak experience, the "masculine protest," "striving for superiority," manifestation of the animus, and, perhaps most centrally, the actualization of the strength archetype. These forces speak of eternal truths.

Chapter 4

PERSONALITY STYLES AND
THE EXPERIENCE OF LIFTING

THUS FAR, we have explored several "paths" of lifting, including their various surface motives, as well as the deeper psychological motives which interact to overdetermine an individual's lifting activity. Beyond all this, there is still another area which I find interesting, that being the relationship between certain personality styles and the experience of lifting. The question which I want to answer is, what is lifting like for some particular types of people?

The key to understanding this question is the idea of "body scripting." A "body script" refers to the messages which a person accepted early in life about how he or she is to act and to be with his or her body. As a child, we all are told what things to do and what things not to do by our parents and other adults who assume a parenting role such as teachers, neighbors, clergy, and so forth.

They may say, "You'd better be careful!" Or, they may say, "Go ahead, and have fun," or even, "Don't be a sissy," implying that one should go ahead and do something beyond one's capability. Not always are these things said so explicitly. They may be implied by what is said. It may be an interesting experiment at this point for the reader to pick one of these three examples of script messages and say it aloud to herself or himself several times. Now, sit with that experience for a couple of minutes and feel what the impact is. Remember, imagine yourself as a child being told this message by a parent or other parenting figure. Say it, again, if necessary. Feel the impact. Now, do the same with one of the other two messages. When you have explored the impact of that one sufficiently, try the third message. This simple experiment may give you a feel for how body scripting happens.

49

The script message may have been repeated over and over. The exact wording may have changed, but the theme may have been presented many times. The variations on the theme may include non-verbal as well as verbal messages. A grimace, a smile and an approving nod, or a mocking look of disgust in response to a child's body play could carry the same meaning as the verbal messages which I suggested above. The non-verbal messages may actually have had a stronger impact than the messages spoken. The important factor is what meaning the child makes of the messages, verbal and non-verbal. Is the meaning one of caution, support, or dare?

Sometimes these rules are given to us with enough force, or with enough threat of punishment or actual punishment, that we record them indelibly. **The organized sum of the rules about our body behavior constitutes our body script.** The script may be more or less unconscious, but is followed nonetheless. So, it is as if each of us is playing out a part which is called for by our particular body script. For some, it is a lifelong script written in early childhood. For others, it is a revised script, the revisions coming about through impactful life experiences, either positive or negative.

The body script is one facet of the more encompassing "life script." Because life is embodied, the body script is a necessary facet of the life script, and is reflective of the larger script. To the extent that the messages accepted are in support of one's aliveness and growth, the script is life enhancing or "biopositive." To the extent that those messages are toxic and not in support of aliveness and growth, the script is deadening or "bionegative."

In the quest to understand the psychological dynamics of the human being, many typologies have been developed. Each one attempts to classify people into several "types" and delineate the characteristics of each. This approach has been of immense value, but also has some serious limitations, not the least of which is that no individual is a pure type. I want to avoid this trap of trying to fit people into neat compartments by acknowledging this limitation of "typing" people, and by emphasizing, instead, personal "styles" which reflect certain body scripts. I want to discuss three major styles of "living one's body." One style is based on a biopositive body script, and the other two are based on bionegative body scripts. These three styles can best be thought of as the middle region (biopositive body script) and the two extreme regions (bionegative body scripts) of a continuum. The styles represented in these three regions may be called the "phobic" style (bionegative), the "self-actualizing" style (biopositive), and the "impulsive" style (bionegative).

Let us explore, first, the **self-actualizing style.** The self-actualizing style is an expression of a natural urge, as discussed in earlier sections of this book. The natural urge to realize one's potential is supported by a biopositive body script. This self-actualizing body script calls for a living of one's body, the experience of being alive and embodied. A person who lives her or his body uses body sensations as input for perceptual and cognitive processes, has a high level of body awareness, experiences the locus of self in the body, experiences high levels of sensual pleasure, and takes care of the body, using it fully, but neither damaging it through misuse nor allowing it to deteriorate through disuse. The lived body is regarded with an attitude of respect and excitement. The script is **"Use your body."**

The person with this script which gives permission for, and supports the use of the body, tends to live passionately. This means to feel strongly. It also means to respond to the natural urge for experience. Experience comes from expanding into the world, from going out and beyond what is familiar and certain. This means the willingness to take reasonable risks.

And, now, to address the question of how someone with this self-actualizing style approaches lifting weights. This person's "Use your body" script calls for the realizing of potential. This person will enjoy using her or his body and will find deep satisfaction in physical progress. Each gain in strength or size or definition will bring meaning and pleasure to this lifter. He or she will have respect for the body's real limits and the actual dangers of lifting, and so will exercise appropriate care and caution. This person will probably appreciate the nature of her or his "growing edge" and work near it, neither wasting time with workouts which are too easy nor unnecessarily risking injury by forcing beyond a limit. Respect for the limits and excitement about the activity of lifting, as well as its results, make this style the one which most often bears the most fruit. This person enjoys her or his workouts and makes the most of them, since the body script supports pleasure in physical activity.

The lifter who has a self-actualizing style is likely to lift with care and awareness. The "Use your body" script invites a tuning into one's embodied self with an attention to body sensations. This lifter will value body sensations as a rich source of information as well as a source of pleasure. To lift with care and awareness is an expression of discipline.

In terms of motive, the lifter with a "Use your body" script will tend not to lift because of a "Should" or even a "Have to in order to," but will lift out of a genuine "Want," or as a path of growth. He or she would not feel driven to lift. Instead, his or her lifting would flow out of a genuine desire to lift. The natural urge for body experience, body use, is supported by a body script which allows for the actualization of that urge.

In contrast to this self-actualizing style, the **phobic style** comes from a bionegative body script. More specifically, this body script is **"Disuse your body."** In this case the natural urge for self-actualization is perverted into an urge to avoid. Those who express this phobic style retreat in anxiety from their growing edge, afraid of discomfort, pain, embarrassment, and the "too muchness" of a life fully lived. This phobic style defines the timid and the shy, the spectators of life.

If the "Disuse your body" script is extreme, the person so oriented is not likely even to walk through the gym door, let alone chalk her or his hands. The result is an undeveloped body or a body showing muscular atrophy. If the severity of this body script is not so extreme, the person may lift, but in a manner reflective of the "Disuse your body" script. The core symptom of a lifter with this script is a lack of vigorous and sustained effort. Such a person shows a phobic reaction to discomfort, let alone pain. Therefore, he or she will avoid muscle burns and painful exertions, and eschew post workout muscle soreness. In order to avoid these discomforts, this lifter will tend to use workout routines which lack sufficient intensity. These less than optimally intense workouts leave this lifter in the region far shy of her or his growing edge. Rather than seeking and tolerating the discomfort of burning and sore muscles, knowing that these are hallmarks of muscular growth, this person will use physical discomfort as a tocsin to slow down, ease off, or stop.

We can recognize a complex or pattern in the lifter who has a "Disuse your body" script. First, workouts lack optimal intensity. This is accomplished by using a combination of weights which are too light, too few sets, sometimes too few exercises per workout, and sometimes rest periods between sets which are too long. Second, the strength development or body development in evidence seems small relative to the length of time the person has been lifting. Third, this lifter expresses how much he or she hates to work out. Often this is expressed by relief when a workout is over. Fourth, many of these lifters drop out, not sustaining interest for more than a few months. In a word, the lifter who has a "Disuse your body" script is undertrained.

The lifter having a "Disuse your body" script is most likely to lift from a motive of "I Should." Being phobic about vigorous physical activity, discomfort, or pain, this lifter does not really want to lift. He or she is doing so because of an external "should," not because of an internal desire. So, he or she may be compliant, but his or her heart is not in it. He or she may feel guilty about missing a workout, or feel relieved at having gotten out of one. But, he or she would neither long to work out nor feel a loss at a missed opportunity with the weights. This lifter, having a phobic style, is not a disciplined lifter. Compliant, at times, but disciplined, no.

The other toxic body script which is relevant here is **"Misuse your body."** This dictates an **impulsive style.** When this script is operating, the person tends to ignore actual limits and real dangers, and to push beyond the growing edge. We might call this person the fool. Her or his pushing of the limits without adequate circumspection and caution inevitably results in some degree of self-destruction. "Look before you leap" has little meaning to the person scripted to misuse her or his body. Such a person tends to act on impulse, her or his action not benefiting from adequate awareness.

The lifter who has a "Misuse your body" script may at first glance be impressive. He or she may be displaying a good, high intensity workout, carried out with enthusiasm and vigor. A real workout animal, it appears that this lifter is an example of what lifting weights is supposed to be. On closer examination, however, it can be discerned that this lifter is overdoing. In her or his quest for development, undermined by a script which calls for abuse of the body, he or she will tend to do some combination of using weights which are too heavy for performing the exercises correctly, using too many sets, using too many exercises per workout, not resting sufficiently between sets, and working out too frequently, not allowing the body adequate time to recuperate. In a word, this lifter is overtrained.

In addition to overtraining, the lifter with this impulsive style is likely to try most anything. It has been said that "fools rush in where angels fear to tread," and so it is with such a lifter. This is the lifter who may walk up to the new machine, drop the pin to the lowest position on the weight stack, and try to lift the whole stack first try! Likewise, he or she may pick up the barbell someone else has been using and try to duplicate the lift without a warm-up.

The impulsive lifter, because of the underlying script which calls for abuse of the body, tends to ignore pain as a danger signal. He or she may not recognize the difference between muscle burns and muscle soreness which are hallmarks of muscle growth and the sharp pains which warn of tearing in the muscles and tendons. This lifter recites in slogan fashion, "No pain, no gain," as he or she takes two more aspirin tablets and picks up the barbell again, to "work through the pain."

The lifter of impulsive style is not a disciplined lifter. Again, to the casual observer, this lifter may appear disciplined. But he or she is driven to lift. This driven quality is revealed on closer observation. He or she pushes and forces beyond what is reasonable. The over-intensity of this lifter bespeaks both a driveness and an underlying motive of "I Have to in order to...." He or she is unreasonably goal directed. This lifter is willing to sacrifice personal well-being and to take foolish risks in the driven pursuit of the goal.

One of the frequent results of the impulsive style is, of course, injury. Another, which is not quite so blatant is overtraining. Both of these results are thoroughly consistent with script of "Misuse your body." **Overtraining is subtle abuse.**

There are several symptoms of overtraining which can appear in various combinations. First, with respect to workouts, the lifter may experience a lack of progress, or even regressions. After a period of good progress, the overtrained lifter may be stuck on a plateau. For several workouts or several weeks, poundages do not increase, or size is not gained. Or, worse, poundages actually decrease or size is lost! So, alarmed at the loss, the lifter works harder, only to exacerbate the problem and possibly inflict an injury. Closely related to this halt in progress is another symptom of overtraining — aversion to working out. The lifter may find that he or she doesn't feel like working out, or may even begin to dread workouts. So, the overtrained lifter pushes herself or himself to pick up the iron.

Other symptoms of overtraining affect the lifter in her or his life in general. One of the most common is a feeling of chronic tiredness and fatigue. The lifter has that feeling of being "worn out," which doesn't go away. To make matters worse, there is often an accompanying disturbance of sleep. This may take the form of difficulty in getting to sleep, waking up during the night with difficulty in getting back to sleep, or restless sleep. So, the fatigued lifter may have difficulty getting a good night's sleep, further adding to her or his tiredness.

There may also be symptoms of nervousness and irritability. The lifter may feel "jumpy" and have difficulty relaxing. He or she may get irritated easily and feel a very low tolerance for the common daily frustrations. This may strain one's relationships with family and friends.

A physiological symptom of this "keyed up" state is an elevated pulse rate. A monitoring of one's resting pulse may reveal that it is more rapid than usual, and that this elevated rate persists.

If overtraining continues, the symptoms can escalate to the point that one actually feels sick. The symptoms become flu-like, with a feeling of being "bone tired," aching all over, weakness, and a general sense of feeling bad. This overall malaise is usually reflected in one's eyes. They will look dull, without sparkle, and without energy.

The symptoms of overtraining reflect a state of overwork and not enough rest. The muscle overloading — muscle repair and the mental concentration — mental rest balances have been disrupted. Good workouts require hard muscular effort and hard mental concentration. This depletes the entire organism. Rest is necessary to allow muscle repair, mental freshness for working out, and the overall re-establishment of organismic homeostasis or balance. There is a price to pay for not respecting that balance and the rhythm of working out and resting which will maintain that balance.

In the gym, we call this overtraining. In the workplace it is called overwork, and in the professions it is referred to as "burnout." In each case, it results from a disrespect for one's own individual psychobiological rhythms. And, beneath this disrespect for one's self, a motive of "I Have to in order to..." is usually found. Rather than doing what one "Wants" to do, one does what he or she believes "Has to" be done in the service of pursuing some image. This is a situation of attempted self-image actualizing rather than self-actualizing. "I have to push, push, push if I'm ever going to have legs the size of Platz." Sorry, that is not the "Way."

The overtrained lifter may look more impressive and lift more impressively than her or his counterpart at the other extreme, the undertrained lifter previously discussed. Neither of these lifters will develop optimally, however. Both are living out a bionegative body script. With the "Disuse your body" script come undertraining and underdevelopment. With the "Misuse your body" script come overtraining and impulsive actions which lead to "staleness" and injury. In both cases, the scripts show negative regard for the body. The "Use your body" script calls for a positive regard and living of the body. The choice is to participate in an embodied life, to shrink from life (disuse the body), or to be the careless fool, burned out or broken down (misuse the body).

The self-actualizing style calls for a constant, exquisite awareness. The path is narrow, with a steep descent to either side. Getting off the path means easy descent to the side of misuse or the side of disuse. To follow the path of disciplined living is to traverse the razor's edge.

Figure 5
Symptoms of Overtraining

In the gym: 1. Loss of enthusiasm for working out.

2. Aversion to working out.

3. Cessation of progress.

4. Loss of previous gains.

In general: 1. Tiredness, fatigue.

2. Sleep disturbance.

3. Nervousness, irritability.

4. Elevated resting pulse.

5. Flu-like symptoms.

Figure 6
Body Script, Personality Style, and Training

"Disuse your body." (Bionegative body script) (Perverted urge)	"Use your body." (Biopositive body script) (Natural urge)	"Misuse your body." (Bionegative body script) (Perverted urge)
Phobic style (Shy and timid)	Self-actualizing style (Passionate)	Impulsive style (Impulsive and foolish)
Undertrain (Atrophy or underdevelopment) (Too far from growing edge) (Undisciplined)	Train optimally (Optimal development) (At growing edge) (Disciplined)	Overtrain (Staleness or injury) (Beyond growing edge) (Undisciplined)
"I Should" motive	"I Want to" or "Path of growth" motive	"I Have to" motive

(For a detailed and more thorough discussion of the theory of body scripting and its relationship to psychological patterns, I recommend my earlier book *The Body in Psychotherapy,* listed in the references of *Not Just Pumping Iron.*)

Chapter 5

APOLLONIAN AND DIONYSIAN
ORIENTATIONS

ONE OF THE most heated debates in the iron world in recent
years has been the debate over equipment. Specifically, the controversy has been framed as "free-weights" versus "machines." The pro-
ponents of free-weights (barbells and dumbbells) have argued that they
are superior for the maximum development of strength and physique,
they allow greater variety of exercises, and they develop coordination
beyond what machines afford. The other camp, those who champion
machines, argue that machines are safer to use, more nearly insure that
any given exercise is performed correctly, and create exercises which
work certain muscles at angles which free-weights cannot. But the
strongest argument put forth by the "high tech" machine companies is
that these machines provide the most efficient development of muscular
strength known.

In order to understand the arguments presented on both sides of the
debate, one must understand how the various pieces of equipment work.
They all have the same purpose, namely, to provide resistance during an
exercise movement and to provide a means of increasing that resistance
over time as the lifter grows stronger. This is in accord with the "overload principle" touched upon in an earlier chapter. To state the principle
simply, when a muscle is worked against a resistance which is greater
than that to which it is accustomed (i.e., "overloaded"), it will increase in
strength in order to accommodate the increased demand. In other
words, overload a muscle and it will become accustomed to the new demand. To keep the muscle growing, keep overloading it, with appropriate time intervals and nutritional requirements for its recuperation. The
various pieces of equipment differ in the type of resistance which they

59

provide and in the way that they change the level of resistance. The most important criterion is that the apparatus provides for progressive resistance exercise.

It is interesting to look at the evolution of weightlifting equipment. The first systematic attempt at progressive resistance training in Western culture was made in ancient Greece by Milo of Crotona. At least, so goes the legend. Milo picked a male calf and hoisted it on his shoulders daily. As the calf grew in weight, Milo grew in strength, until one day he was able to lift the grown bull. Whether the details of this legend are true or not, the legend does inform us that by the time of the ancient Greeks the basic principle of progressive resistance training for strength was known. If Milo used a bull, it seems likely others tried other animals. So, a growing animal may have been the first progressive resistance apparatus used systematically. Although this has been tried in modern times, it has been more of a stunt, a novelty. I have yet to visit a gym which keeps livestock. Beyond the obvious inconvenience, there are other major limitations to such an apparatus. Most notably, there is a severe limit to the number of exercises which can be done with a large lively animal. More subtle, but important, is the fact that a large animal such as a bull grows from lightweight calfhood to huge bullhood at a rate which exceeds the rate of its lifter's growth in strength. Therefore, it can be used only during a limited period of its growth. Animals, as progressive resistance apparatus, are clearly passe, eclipsed by more convenient equipment.

With the progressive resistance principle established, thanks to Milo's bovine demonstration, no doubt other people used the principle with various kinds of makeshift exercise equipment. Perhaps stones of progressive sizes were collected for lifting and tossing. Cannon balls, being more comfortable to hold, may have replaced stones. In time, someone may have thought to put a handle on a cannon ball, and the kettlebell was invented. Thinking it would be easier to "handle" a pair of cannon balls, the dumbbell evolved. And, as soon as someone wanted to do a two hand lift with one heavy dumbbell, the handle was extended, and the barbell came into being. These early pieces of equipment were known as globe dumbbells and barbells or spherical dumbbells and barbells because of the shape of the weighted end pieces. The metal spheres or globes were sometimes solid, sometimes hollow. The hollow spheres could, of course, be larger for a given amount of weight, and would therefore look more impressive when lifted. As I mentioned in a previous chapter, other heavy objects were lifted in the early strength shows — anvils, cannon, platforms loaded with people, automobiles, or animals, and sledge hammers. Sometimes barbells were constructed from heavy wheels or from barrels which were then filled with some weighty content.

For the strength showmen, all of these apparati were important, and the more dramatic the better. But for the non-professional, the man, and more rarely, the woman who wanted to engage in the new "physical culture," the spherical dumbbells and barbells became the popular equipment. Free-hand calisthenics and calisthenics with fixed weight equipment such as Indian clubs and medicine balls began to be supplanted in the new physical culture circles by progressive resistance exercise, made possible by graduated sets of dumbbells and barbells. Exercise routines were pretty much standardized, based on the publication of a book by Theodor Siebert in Germany in 1907 (Rasch, 1966). (Interestingly, Siebert's exercises constitute the core of beginning lifting routines even today.)

In addition to making progressive resistance exercise practical for many people, barbells and dumbbells provide a degree of standardization which was necessary for competitive lifting to develop. As part of their shows, the early strong men often put forth a challenge to members of the audience to step forth and equal their demonstrated feats. The feats, however, often involved odds and ends of non-standardized equipment, perhaps of unknown weight, and non-standardized ways of lifting (or bending and breaking, as in the case of horseshoes and chains, respectively). This, of course, gave the show person a distinct advantage in that the person who took up the challenge, in most cases, would not have had the opportunity to practice with this unique equipment.

An improvement of spherical weights came with the use of lead shot to load the hollow spheres to desired poundages. This was another step towards a standardized apparatus so much needed for lifting competition. With shot loaded spherical barbells it was easier for someone to attempt someone else's best lift at another place and another time. A weight could be reported and a challenger could put his barbell on the scale and add lead shot until a desired weight was reached. The loaded sphere also made it easier to practice progressive resistance training in that fewer barbells and dumbbells were required. One could increase the weight of an existing barbell or dumbbell by adding lead shot as he or she became stronger, rather than having to construct or purchase a heavier barbell or dumbbell with each significant increase in strength.

Loaded spherical weights were used in Olympic competition as late as the 1924 games in Paris. That year lifters had a choice of using these or of using the new disc equipped barbell (Gaudreau, 1975).

The clatter of barbell plates was the death knell for the spherical barbell. The invention of the barbell which used discs or plates meant that one piece of equipment would conveniently serve for many. One adjustable barbell could be quickly and easily loaded to any desired weight. This meant that a person who could not afford to equip a home gym with several spherical barbells of different sizes, or who didn't want to perform a tedious operation of weighing, loading, and unloading a hollow sphere with lead shot, could now purchase one apparatus which would meet a wide variety of exercise needs, at an affordable price. The mechanics of progressive resistance exercise were now simple and convenient. In addition, much greater standardization was possible. A group of lifters in competition could all use the same barbell with plates added as needed. That meant that they all used a bar with one diameter, one balance, and one "feel." And, in time, this meant precisely standardized dimensions for competition barbells.

Anyone who has lifted both a solid barbell and an adjustable barbell knows the tremendous difference in the feel. The revolving sleeve or even the revolving plates of an adjustable barbell allow one to make quick movements and changes of direction of movement without feeling that the bar may be wrenched from one's grip. I remember vividly my surprise the first time I lifted a solid spherical barbell. I was warming up for an Olympic style contest being held at an old Turner club in the Midwest. This was sometime in the early 1960s. Among the array of iron in the warmup room was a solid iron barbell. I picked it up, and found it to be a suitable weight for doing some warmup power cleans and presses. So, I lowered it to the floor and did a power clean. To my consternation my wrists bent back painfully as the barbell reached shoulder level. The momentum of the barbell twisted my wrists well past the point where they were accustomed to stopping on a power clean. I knew then why these unwieldy hunks of iron were not any longer the chosen equipment of lifting.

A less dramatic, but equally impressive experience formed the basis of my regard for the solid kettlebell. While teaching a psychotherapy seminar on a Russian ship, the M.S. Kazatstan, I was delighted to learn that there was a gym aboard. The first time I had a chance, I went off excitedly to work out. What I found was a small room with some exercise mats and several assorted solid dumbbells and kettlebells. From pictures which I had seen of early strongmen and strongwomen, I recognized the kettlebells with some sense of mystique. What I found, upon using them, or, more accurately, trying to use them for some one arm curls and one arm presses, was that they were quite uncomfortable. More than just unwieldy, the handles were difficult to grip as the angle of hold shifted during a curl or press. I understand why kettlebells are relegated to the category of antique equipment.

The solid barbell and the kettlebell are items of the past, left along the road of progress as more comfortable and versatile equipment emerged. The solid dumbbell has survived, however. Especially in gyms, where a rack of progressively weighted dumbbells is desirable, the solid ones are often found. There is also a safety factor involved. Whereas, when a barbell is lifted, the bar is intentionally kept parallel to the floor, when dumbbells are lifted, they are intentionally rotated so that the bars have excursions from parallel to the floor to vertical. This means that collars or clamps must be tightly affixed to both ends of the bars if plates are used, to prevent the plates from sliding off. Solid dumbbells avoid the hazard of falling plates from carelessly applied collars or clamps. Some gyms use adjustable dumbbells which have permanently welded collars, thereby preventing falling weights.

Barbells, too, can have permanently affixed collars, thereby creating a safer piece of equipment, while having the advantage of a rotating sleeve, or at least rotating plates. Many gyms have racks of such barbells in progressive weights. More and more, though, the best gyms provide Olympic or power bars with a large assortment of various sized plates and heavy duty collars.

An interesting side note is that in an occasional advertisement or store display the plates are arranged on a barbell from smallest to largest and back to smallest. This symmetrical arrangement is reminiscent of the spherical barbell. It looks almost as if someone sliced the spheres. In fact, I have seen dumbbells whose plates were beveled such that when they were placed on the bars, smallest to largest to smallest, they actually formed spheres! Such arrangements of plates, though not convenient when adjusting barbells, are a reminder of the adjustable barbell's roots.

The adjustable barbell is clearly the quintescence of weightlifting equipment. In its most highly evolved form, the Olympic or power bar, it is balanced and of exactly marked weight. Its balance, its smoothly rotating bar, its precisely located knurling, and its "feel" all contribute to making it the easiest way to lift a given weight. Olympic bars and power bars have a slightly different diameter, the latter being greater, to subtly accommodate those different styles of lifting. Simple in concept, this barbell is evolved and of incredible versatility.

There are various pieces of equipment which are adjuncts to the barbell, and its smaller cohort the dumbbell. Included are squat racks, power racks, flat benches, incline benches, decline benches, and preacher curl benches. All of these are in the service of lifting barbells and dumbbells.

For many years there have been other pieces of equipment which have co-existed with the barbells and dumbbells, and served as either adjuncts or alternatives available for variety. These are the various pulley machines — lat pull, triceps extension, crossover cables, cable row, and so forth — and calf machines. These simple machines, in their earlier versions, were loaded with barbell plates, and in their current versions have built-in weight stacks with a selector pin for selecting the proportion of the weight stack desired. The calf machine is an easier and more comfortable version of doing toe raises with a barbell on one's back. The lat pull is an alternative to the chinning bar and a weight belt on which barbell plates are hung. The other cable systems simply employ a pulley to change the direction of pull so that one can pull down or pull horizontally or pull at some angle in between, rather than being restricted to pulling or pushing a barbell or dumbbells on a vertical plane against gravity. In essence, these machines do nothing that can not be done with a barbell, dumbbells and a chinning bar. They do, however, add interesting variety and some more comfortable alternatives for certain exercises. (Actually, lat pulls and chins do have a subtly different effect, as they involve moving the resistance toward one's stationary body, or moving one's body as the resistance, respectively.)

These machines, however, are not the ones which represent one side of the "free-weights" versus "machines" debate. The machines in the debate are "high tech" machines. The essence of the "high tech" machine is that it involves moving a lever against an automatically variable resistance. Both of these characteristics are important. First, by having a lever to be moved, the machine requires that a particular motion, for which that particular machine is designed, and only that motion, is used. This allows for relative isolation of the muscle group for which the machine is designed. In other words, recruitment of muscles other than those which the machine is designed to exercise, is minimized. "Cheating" on an exercise is made difficult. Second, the automatically variable resistance accommodates the mechanical advantage of the body. When lifting a barbell or dumbbell the level of difficulty varies throughout the range of motion of the exercise. In lifting parlance, there is a "sticking point." So, the weight lifted is limited by the weight which can be moved through the point of least mechanical advantage. What this means is that the muscle does not get exercised maximally throughout its entire range of motion, but only in the zone of least mechanical advantage. In the zones where there is greater mechanical advantage, the muscle may work very little with that weight. By using an automatically variable resistance, the machine provides more resistance in the zones of greater mechanical advantage and less resistance in the zone of least mechanical advantage. In other words, the machine eases up at the sticking point in the exercise. The result — maximal resistance throughout the full range of motion of the exercise.

Because of this second essential feature of the "high tech" machines, automatically variable resistance, they are referred to as "isokinetic" machines (Riley, 1977). Resistance is automatically varied by several means. Some machines use a cam, some a variable length lever arm, some a hydraulic cylinder, and some a pneumatic cylinder.

The isokinetic machine was invented quite some years ago. The first Nautilus machine was built in 1948, although Nautilus equipment was not commercially available until 1970. Although many other companies offer isokinetic machines, the Nautilus company has published the most research, done the most advertising, and even set up Nautilus centers, franchised widely. So successful has been their campaign that much of the general public knows of Nautilus, but may be unfamiliar with names such as Bio-Dyne, Camstar, Cybex, Keiser, Maxicam, Polaris, Power-cise, and Universal. The name Nautilus has become as a common noun, used by many as the word to refer to weight training machines, just as names such as Frigidaire, Kodak and Xerox came to be used in lieu of refrigerator, camera and photocopy, respectively. A frequent question asked of me when someone hears that I am a lifter, is, "Do you do Nautilus or free-weights?"

That question reflects the "either/or" controversy. Much of the controversy resulted, I believe, from the public claims made by the representatives of Nautilus. Prior to the advent of commercially available Nautilus equipment, there was no debate about free-weights versus machines. After all, the machines which existed before the isokinetic machines were essentially barbell adjuncts, not machines created to replace free-weights. But with Nautilus, the point was different. Arthur Jones (1977, p. 156), for instance, declared that "Instead of trying to fit human muscles to an imperfect tool, the barbell — Nautilus was an attempt to design perfect tools that would exactly fit the requirements of muscles." Jones was critical of machines which "...merely copy the functions of a barbell," saying some rather inflammatory words, namely, that such machines "...are now about as practical for the purpose of exercise as a horse is for the purpose of transportation" (Jones, 1977, p. 156). If this were not sufficient, Jones (1977, p. 160) went on to say that "Nautilus is the ONLY source of 'total' exercise."

During the height of the Nautilus movement, as Nautilus centers were being established throughout the country, a highly accomplished lifter came forward endorsing the equipment. Some time later, a brother team of well known physique stars added their endorsement. The former star claimed great things for Nautilus equipment, giving many the impression that his massive, defined physique and great strength were the products of Nautilus training.

With all this, Nautilus appeared to many to be the state of the art, and predicted that the barbell would gather dust as it became a relic of the "old," that is, pre-Nautilus days. Other equipment manufacturers boarded the band wagon and emulated Nautilus as closely as patent laws would allow.

So what happened? Why were free-weights not phased out? First of all, the lofty claims of Nautilus did not hold up for hardcore lifters. The softcore lifting public liked the machines. They seemed simple to use, convenient, and efficient for producing some quick gains in overall muscle conditioning. Hardcore lifters sometimes reported that they did not experience as complete a pump from the machines as from free-weights. Whether that was an objective fact or not, it reflected a dissenting opinion about the popular machines. Then came an exposé. The star, who had early on endorsed Nautilus, stepped forward to announce publicly that he had been paid well to endorse Nautilus and that he had actually built his physique using free-weights. In fact, this man had competed in a Mr. America contest prior to even using Nautilus equipment. The fact became realized that exclusive Nautilus training had never produced a champion physique. And, obviously, Olympic style lifters and power lifters must do a major part of their training on the equipment with which they compete, namely the barbell.

What has emerged is the following pattern. Many softcore lifters prefer the machines. As I have said previously, they are safer, easier, and simpler to use than free-weights. The Nautilus training program has proven to be a highly efficient way of muscle conditioning for overall strength, for health and other sports. Hardcore lifters, on the other hand, tend to use a combination of equipment — free-weights **and** machines. When the Nautilus machines are used, however, they are rarely used following the Nautilus training program. For Olympic style lifters and powerlifters the machines, if used at all, are clearly used as adjuncts to the primary free-weight training.

The basic fact of the matter is baldly stated by Daniel P. Riley (1977, p. 97). "The most important consideration...is really personal preference. Remember that it is the **quality** of training (not the equipment) that will provide the greatest increases in muscle strength and mass. Significant gains in strength can be obtained by using any kind of equipment that will overload the muscles."

Of particular interest to us, in the context of the present book, is the psychological reason for the personal preference of equipment. Many lifters enjoy variety and therefore use particular equipment for several weeks or months and then shift to different equipment for a similar period. Such shifts in equipment can stimulate the lifter's interest, infusing workouts with new excitement. So, at the time a lifter is freshly using some new equipment he or she may be very enthusiastic, touting the advantages of that apparatus. But, beyond this transient enthusiasm, there seems to be a personal preference by which lifters gravitate to basic equipment — barbells, dumbbells, and appurtenant apparati — or to high tech equipment.

Having described the essential qualities of the basic equipment and the high tech equipment, let us turn to the essential psychological qualities which predispose one to one type of equipment or the other. In order to understand the predisposition, we can look to two competing world views which have been identified. These two alternative visions appear across cultures, and, although the names used to identify them vary from culture to culture, their elements are consistent. As Sam Keen (1974) has expressed it, in modern times the majority of people have followed the vision which can be named after the Greek god Apollo, whereas a minority have followed the alternate vision which can be identified with the Greek god Dionysus. Earlier writers, including the philosopher Nietzsche have discussed the Dionysian spirit, and Karen Horney, the psychoanalyst, wrote of the Dionysian and Apollonian approaches to experience.

It is precisely this Dionysian-Apollonian split which explains, I believe, not only a lifter's preference for equipment, but her or his style of training. Let me elaborate by first delving into the differences between the two world views.

These two alternative visions are clearly represented by the deified personalities of Apollo and Dionysus. Apollo was the Greek god of light, moderation, reason, truth, order, balance, and boundaries. Dionysus was the Greek god of wine, excess, fantasy, and metamorphosis. He was the only Greek god whose parents were not both divine. Dionysus was sometimes man's blessing, sometimes his curse, as he offered both freedom and ecstatic joy on the one hand, and savage brutality on the other. In one story, for instance, Dionysus took the form of an angry lion. In another, this god of wine turned a group of women mad, causing them to attack and devour their own children. Dionysus could make people merry, quicken their courage, banish their fear, or he could bring on their destruction through drunkenness. He also taught the world about metamorphosis. In the winter his vines were dark and withered, but with spring his vines sprouted forth to spread and grow, eventually yielding the summer and fall harvests of his grapes. The metamorphosis was dramatic, from apparent deadness to exuberant aliveness and abundance. In the Roman empire, Dionysus was known as Bacchus.

In her discussion of the Apollonian and Dionysian tendencies, Karen Horney (Shostrom, 1967) stressed the emphasis of mastery and molding in the former, and surrender and drift in the latter. She saw both of these leanings as natural human "tendencies." So, neither is better nor worse in and of itself, and no one is completely Apollonian or Dionysian. A person will exhibit tendencies in one direction or the other at different times. When exhibiting the Apollonian tendency, a person will emphasize being in charge and in control, and making things happen in the way he or she wishes. The approach is to change the world in the ways I wish. The opposite is the case with the Dionysian tendency. Rather than exerting her or his will to mold the world, the person disposed toward a Dionysian approach will give in to what is, and allow the world to take her or him away. This is a surrender of personal will to the will of the world around her or him. The Apollonian tendency is to conquer the universe, tame the wilds and make this a "better" world. The Dionysian tendency is to get in harmony with the universe, experience the wilds, and come to a relaxed acceptance of the world as it is.

Less poetic and more baldly descriptive of these tendencies are the words "scientist" and "artist." The scientist is more Apollonian in her or his view and approach to life. Description, understanding, and prediction of the world and its manifestations are the goals of the pure scientist. For the applied scientist, the goal is to use the insights of the pure scientist to control various phenomena of the world. The artist is more oriented around appreciative observation and pleasing representation of the world through various media. Rather than change the world, the artist tries to illuminate and reflect it with an esthetic light. The scientist ultimately wants to effect a change in the world. The artist wants to create an esthetic experience of the world.

Paralleling the terms Apollonian and Dionysian, Carl Jung (1970) wrote of the "logos" and "eros" principles. The logos principle is one of objective interest in the world. When one takes an objective view of something, putting aside emotional and personal subjective considerations he or she is operating in accordance with the logos principle. Historically, in the West, this has been identified more often with a "masculine" orientation. The eros principle is one of psychic relatedness. In other words, this principle is expressed in the subjective, emotional experience of relating to the world. This more intimate mode of experiencing can involve relating to other people, ideas, animals, and even the inanimate world. Jung noted that in the Western view this psychic relatedness is usually seen as "feminine." So, the logos principle corresponds to an Apollonian orientation, while the eros principle is consistent with a Dionysian orientation.

These two world views are discussed in an intriguing way by Robert Pirsig (1974) in his unusual book *Zen and the Art of Motorcycle Maintenance*. The sub-title of his book, "an inquiry into values," provides an accurate insight, for the two world views which we are exploring are statements of some rather basic values. The terms which Pirsig uses are "classical understanding" and "romantic understanding." From the classical position, the world is seen as underlying form. From the romantic position the world is seen in terms of immediate experience. These last statements are quite heady, and beg for some both-feet-on-the-ground explanation by example. Bear with me. Imagine showing a blueprint to two people, one a romantic the other a classicist. The romantic would see it as a thing in itself. He or she would primarily see lines, geometric forms, numbers, symbols. The romantic would tend to see this blueprint as rather uninteresting. For the person of a classical bent, however, some interest would likely be aroused. He or she would recognize that the blueprint is representational. The lines and shapes and symbols represent something else, some underlying form. The romantic sees a blueprint, the classicist sees a representation of a house.

Pirsig elaborated beyond this basic difference between the person of classical and the person of romantic inclination. The mode of the romantic tends to be inspirational, imaginative, creative, and intuitive.

Feelings take priority over facts. Esthetic considerations are rated highly.

The person in the classical mode proceeds in an orderly fashion using reason and laws. More intellectual than emotional in orientation, facts take priority and esthetic considerations are downgraded. The classical mode seeks to control, not merely intuit the meaning of something.

Pirsig correctly identified that persons tend to orient themselves through one of these two modes, and consequently not appreciate people who have chosen the other mode. It is often this difference in orientation which results in people's misunderstanding of each other. This is reflected in many cases when someone says, truthfully, "I can't understand why anyone would want to do that." The fact is, "although motorcycle riding is romantic, motorcycle maintenance is purely classic" (Pirsig, 1974, p. 67). The romantic mode is Dionysian, and the classical mode is Apollonian.

Additional insights into the Apollonian-Dionysian split have been offered by Sam Keen (1974). Referring to the former as the "rational" view and the latter as the "cosmic" view, he identifies them as left-brain and right-brain functions, respectively. (Studies of hemispheric specialization have suggested that the left lobe processes data by sequential analysis of abstract, symbolic "bits." This involves a logical, temporal, cause and effect approach. The right lobe, in contrast, processes data in a holistic, integrative way, providing recognition of patterns. It may be primarily involved in imaging and emotional expression.) The rational view values work above play, whereas the cosmic view takes the opposite priority, valuing play above work. If work and play are the contents which differ, respectively, within the value systems of the rational view and the cosmic view, then the styles are also different. From the rational view, it is efficiency which is sought. In the cosmic view it is ecstasy. Efficient work versus ecstatic play define the poles of the rational view — cosmic view continuum.

I hope I have provided an accurate, precise, and efficient intellectual understanding of the Apollonian and Dionysian orientations, for those of you who are, yourselves, Apollonian in your world view. For those of a more Dionysian persuasion, I hope to have provided an esthetically pleasing image and inspirational picture with which you can feel yourself relate. A summary is offered in Figure 7.

How do people of each of these orientations approach the lifting of weights? Their differing world views are, I believe, clearly expressed in their training approaches. First, an example from the popular culture

Figure 7

Apollonian and Dionysian Orientations

Apollonian	Dionysian
mastery and molding	surrender and drift

Scientist	Artist

Logos	Eros
objective interest	psychic relatedness
"masculine"	"feminine"

Classical	Romantic
order	inspirational
reason	imaginative
law	creative
control	intuitive
underlying form	immediate experience
facts predominate	feelings predominate
unadorned	esthetic
intellectual	emotional

Rational	Cosmic
efficiency	ecstasy
work	play
left-brain	right-brain

with which many readers will be familiar. In the movie, "Rocky IV," the Apollonian and Dionysian approaches to training were beautifully and graphically depicted. It was not hardcore lifting which was involved, to be sure, but it was hard, serious training for competition which included strength building. In the film, Rocky Balboa trained from a Dionysian orientation. The contrast between his Dionysian inspired training and his opponent's Apollonian guided training is most explicit.

Visualize the two training scenes. Rocky trained outdoors and in a barn. His Russian opponent, Ivan Drago, trained in a high tech laboratory/gym. In order to develop endurance, Rocky ran through knee deep snow, jumped rope, and ran up a mountain. Ivan ran on an indoor track, stepped on a climbing machine, and ran on a treadmill. During all of these he was wired with electrodes in order to feed physiological data into a computer for analysis and input to his trainers. Rocky worked his abdominals by doing sit ups while hanging from the barn loft by his knees, his trainer holding his lower legs. He also did standing twists while holding a heavy ox yoke on his back. Ivan did abdominal crunches on a machine. While Rocky used a speed bag, Ivan used a machine which looked like the pedals of a bicycle, rotating them rapidly with his hands. For leg strength, Rocky made himself a beast of burden, pulling a sled full of people along a snow covered road, and carrying a heavy timber on his back. In his laboratory/gym, Ivan used a sled machine. Rocky used chin-ups to work his biceps. Ivan sat at a curling machine, carefully isolating his biceps. Rocky strengthened his upper body by chopping down a large tree, cutting it into logs with a hand saw, and splitting the logs into kindling with an axe. He rigged an overhead pulley with a net full of rocks on one end of the rope for doing "cable" triceps extensions. And, finally, he loaded a two wheeled cart with people and did military presses by the wagon tongues. Meanwhile, Ivan was performing heavy power cleans and military presses with a gleaming, chrome-plated Olympic bar.

Surrounding Rocky was a motley crew of trainers, including the crude, but likable imp of a man, Pauly. They joked, kidded, and fussed with each other. In contrast, the training laboratory of Ivan Drago was peopled by serious, rather coldly intellectual people wearing white laboratory coats and wielding clip boards. The societies of the two training facilities showed marked contrast.

Not only were the facilities, equipment, and training personnel in contrast, but the training attitudes were also widely disparate. For Ivan and his trainers, training was a serious job to be performed with a scientific efficiency. Training proceeded without emotion, aimed at the molding of a fighting machine. This was strictly "masculine," the linear pursuit of a goal of mastery. Rocky, although committed to defeating the Russian, took a more playful approach. He was emotional, feeling the remorse of his friend's death in the ring at the hands of Ivan Drago. He felt hatred for, and fear of the Russian machine. As ironic as it sounds, at first, Rocky's approach was more a manifestation of the "feminine." Both his training and his relationships with his trainers were thoroughly infused with emotion. Rocky was a colorful, feeling, playful human. He trained through inspiration, guided by his intuition and the feedback of his immediate experience. His physical pain and exhaustion were his guides, not digital readouts from a biofeedback computer. His entire quest was that of a romantic, giving it his best shot in the face of uncertainty, and surrendering to whatever outcome.

In Rocky's corner was the power of the eros principle. He was the personification of the romantic artist. Ivan Drago, the classical scientist, took his power from the principle of the logos.

From the graphic example given to us by the folk hero, Rocky, we can recognize the manifestations of Apollonian and Dionysian orientations in the world of lifting weights. First, in terms of style of training, the lifter with an Apollonian view would tend to look for the latest scientifically based routine, and follow it carefully. This lifter wants results, wants to define a goal clearly and move toward that goal with maximum efficiency. From the training research come the principles of scientific training. So, this lifter makes those principles into rules, and trains by the rules. He or she wants to be master of her or his body and to mold it into the desired form. Training is serious, and is undertaken as hard work to be done. When not lifting, considerable time may be devoted to studying the relevant books and magazines. This lifter eagerly opens the latest issue of her or his favorite "muscle mag" to see what the latest research shows, what the latest training method is, or what secret exercise is being revealed by the current Mr. Olympia or reigning weightlifting champion. In the gym he or she can be seen between sets recording in detail in a notebook the sets, reps and weights of the workout in progress.

Liking to bring order and precision into the lifting endeavor, the Apollonian lifter will tend to keep careful records of progress. For the competitive lifter this means recording maximum lifts. For the bodybuilder it means recording carefully taken measurements. The measurements may even be entered into a formula, such as the Willoughby Anthropometric Sex Differentiation Formula (Willoughby and Weaver, 1947), to derive an overall score. The improvement of such a formula-derived score may be the training goal.

Just as the lifter of Apollonian vision studies the books and magazines for the newest breakthrough in exercise routines, he or she will seek out diet advice. This lifter will tend to follow strictly a precisely defined diet. Calorie charts and food scales carefully calibrated in grams become mealtime companions. And, no food tastes too bad or is too exotic if it is endorsed by a champion. In her or his larder, food supplements abound.

In terms of aerobic exercise, this lifter will gravitate towards a high tech machine which may give a digital readout or even a computerized voice calling forth current pulse rate, calories being used per unit of time, adherence to pre-selected aerobic training range, elapsed time, and time remaining. Apollonian oriented lifters are likely to be familiar with punching in their data on a computer keyboard as they mount a Dynavit or Lifecycle machine and start pedaling. They delight at the sense of control and precision afforded by the high tech machine which they pedal, row, tread, or climb.

By now the trend is clear. It will come as no surprise that with regard to lifting equipment itself, it is the Apollonian orientation which leads one to high tech machines. The developers of these machines and the instructors who have these available proclaim their efficiency in muscle conditioning and growth. These promises of efficiency mean maximum results for one's efforts, based on the use of scientifically designed and tested equipment. Beyond these verbalized promises, the machines, themselves, present an image of state of the art technology. The epitome of this image, at this time, is the machine which monitors the lifting and "coaches" either through an electronic readout, a television monitor, or even a computer generated voice. All of this appeals highly to those who have an Apollonian vision.

For the lifter who takes a Dionysian view, the lifting experience is quite different. Such a lifter tends toward "instinct" training. Although this term is frequently used, actually it is a misnomer. An instinct is an innate impulse or propensity. What we are talking about, here, is not in-born. When "instinct" is used to describe a training approach, what is meant is training guided by immediate experience and intuition. Rather than following a prescribed exercise routine, the "instinct" trainer does what feels right. With no pre-determined exercises, sets, repetitions, or weights, he or she enters the gym to lift as her or his inner voice says. He or she will intuit what to do, and allow her or his intuition to be informed by the feel of the lifting as it happens. "Today, I feel like working my legs, hard. I think I'll start with squats. ...That weight feels light; I'll bet I can do ten more pounds. ...I'm tired; that's enough for today. I'll be sore to-. morrow. Good workout!" This is the way the process of working out is for the man or woman of Dionysian vision. Workouts are not by the book and they are not pre-set. No two workouts will be alike. Workouts evolve as they go along, guided by hunches, intuitive impulses, and the feel of the weights. This training approach tends to be playful. The play may be hard, but nonetheless it is play for this lifter. Given this playful quality, and the willingness to follow hunches and intuitive impulses, some workouts unfold as highly imaginative and creative. Exciting discoveries can be made. "I wonder what would happen if I superset donkey calf raises and lunges. I have a hunch that will really work. I'll try it."

The Dionysian inspired lifter may come to experience a mystical quality to her or his workout. Focusing on the moment to moment experience of lifting brings one into an intense and intimate relationship with one's self and between one's self and the exercise equipment. Objective realities — poundages, repetitions, goals — fade into a pale background as the physical sensations of the moment leap into a bright, vivid figure of perceptual awareness. The here-and-now experience — the heaving of one's chest in grabbing for air, the burn in one's muscles, the heat in one's entire body, the overall sense of strain, the sense of focus and singleness of purpose in getting the weight up — can be one of ecstasy. There is a certain esthetic pleasure realized here. The bar and I, in motion, in our dance, create an esthetic experience. The bar and I come into an intimate relationship, a level of psychic relatedness emerges. In this moment, emotion is strong and I surrender to an experience beyond words.

I have had this experience of ecstasy and surrender often, while lifting. Most often it has been while performing a maximum or near maximum lift. As best I can describe it, it is as if the rest of the world fades away, and all that matters is the immediate experience of myself with the bar. We are, for a short time, the center of the cosmos. Barbell-and-I are one, in motion. (I will discuss this further in Part II, where I will address the use of a trance state in the enhancement of lifting performance.)

In expressing the product of lifting, the bodybuilder of Dionysian persuasion will prefer to pose. It is the free-form display of physique which thrills her or him, not objective measures of the tape, body calipers, and scales. Those are cold. This bodybuilder wants something warmer and more inspiring of emotional response. In a phrase, this bodybuilder seeks an emotionally moving esthetic experience.

The training table of the lifter inspired by the Dionysian view is not set in accord with any precisely planned diet. It is, however, met with a hearty appetite. Just as this lifter approaches her or his workouts intuitively, he or she also eats with intuition as a guide. Hunches and cravings dictate the timing and the content of meals.

For aerobic exercise, the lifter of Dionysian vision is most likely to jog, swim, or play some active game. Rather than gravitating to high tech aerobic equipment, he or she will do something more playful, preferably outdoors. Again, the "feel" of the activity will be the feedback for deciding when enough is enough.

The obvious conclusion to this portrait of the lifter of Dionysian orientation is a preference for free-weights. It is free-weights which allow the variety of lifting which this lifter seeks. The number of exercises and variations which are possible with an adjustable barbell and either a rack of dumbbells or a pair of adjustable dumbbells truly staggers, as well as creatively challenges the imagination. Free-weights offer freedom and almost limitless possibilities, just what the Dionysian lifter needs to indulge her or his playful, intuitive, imaginative approach to lifting. If any doubt exists about the versatility of free-weights, a perusal of Bill Pearl's (1978) *Keys to the Inner Universe* will surely prove convincing. He offers 514 pages of exercises, two to four exercises per page!

If the lifter of Apollonian vision seeks efficient, scientifically based training with high tech equipment, her or his brothers and sisters of Dionysian vision seek the romantic experience of barbell curls in the backyard on a sunny day, followed by a quart of milk. Both visions are valid; both "work." Either vision, extreme and not blended with the other view, has limitations. Both the hyper-serious work of the extreme Apollonian and the too casual play of the Dionysian fall short of the balanced, integrated world view which would best guide the lifter to realize her or his potential. Both efficiency and ecstasy have value in human experience.

Figure 8

Apollo and Dionysus in the Gym

Apollo	Dionysus
Isokinetic machines	Free-weights
Dynavit machine or Lifecycle	Jog
Precise diet	Hearty appetite
Willoughby formula	Posing
Training by the rules, based on scientific principles	"Instinct" training, based on intuition and immediate experience
Error of being hyper-serious	Error of being too casual
Work	Play

Persons often tend to pursue one or the other of these two visions. This leads to a misunderstanding of lifters of the other view, and, perhaps, a lack of appreciation of the value of the other view. To the lifter of Apollonian vision, the lifter disposed to the Dionysian view may seem to lack seriousness, to be frivolous, to lack in technical knowledge, and to be inefficient, if not ineffective, in her or his use of antequated equipment and routines. From the opposite view, the lifters of Apollonian orientation may seem too serious, dull, too rigid in adherence to plans and routines, and too uptight about efficient results from those ridiculous machines that they strap themselves into, to perform strict, mechanical exercises lacking in romantic appeal.

Perhaps bodybuilding is in essence a pursuit of a Dionysian vision. Dionysus, as god of metamorphosis, instructed mortals in the miracle of transformation. He also offered instruction in fantasy. The bodybuilder pursues a vision. It is her or his fantasy to undergo dramatic metamorphosis, to evolve from physical ordinariness or a withered condition to a dramatic extraordinariness of physique, a condition of exuberant aliveness and physical abundance. In this incredible metamorphosis the bodybuilder follows the lead of Dionysus. Remember, though, Dionysus not only could usher in a state of merriment and heightened courage, but he could bring men and women to destruction through their drunkenness. So it is with the bodybuilder. Dionysus was god of excess. Too often, the bodybuilder becomes drunk with her or his sprouting forth and runs headlong down a path of excess. The results can be physical grotesqueness, through excessive muscular hypertrophy, permanent injury, or even death. These serious results can accrue from the foolish use of steroids, the contemporary grape of destruction. It is at the point of joyous ecstasy and growth that Apollo is welcome. He, being the god of reason, moderation, and limits, can temper the basically Dionysian pursuit of bodybuilding and bring a balance.

So, if bodybuilding is basically a response to the call of Dionysus, then Apollonian values serve to keep reasonable order in the answer to that call. A balanced world view allows merriment and metamorphosis, within the light of reason, exuberance and abundance, within the boundaries of balance, ecstasy with efficiency.

Chapter 6

THE MEANING OF PAIN,
INJURY AND COMPETITION

"ENDURING AGONY is where it's at." I heard Larry Scott proclaim this several years ago at one of his bodybuilding seminars. Presented as a basic axiom of bodybuilding, his proclamation has stuck with me. In another seminar, I heard Bill Pearl say, "Something must hurt all the time if you are a bodybuilder." These immortals of the iron world were calling attention to two applications of the weight lifter's mantra, "No pain, no gain." (In some forms of Eastern meditation, a simple sound or phrase is repeated over and over. The carefully selected sound or phrase is chosen for its deeper meaning and its ability to resonate in the spiritual centers of the meditator. It is known as a "mantra.") By now, well known to lifters and even many non-lifters, this mantra contains the essential guide to the activity of weight training. But, as well known and oft heard as it is — No pain, no gain — the mantra is not always understood. So, let us delve into its meaning, the very meaning of pain, for the lifter.

Growth often involves pain. Not always. But, often. This fact is reflected in our language by the traditional phrase, "growing pains." At the very least, growth is disruptive. Growth requires change, and change, by definition, involves a restructuring. To restructure, first requires a destructuring. The existing structure must, to some degree, be destructured in order that the new structure can be created. The sequence of growth can be conceptualized as a process of destroying the old structure in order to allow the reconstituting of a more advanced structure. Pain accompanies both of these stages.

An example may clarify this growth sequence and the relationship of pain to that sequence. Although these general principles apply to growth in all realms — physical, mental, emotional, spiritual — I will use an example in the physical realm. Consider the basic phenomenon of bodybuilding. The bodybuilder has a muscle of a particular size, shape, and strength. Wanting to grow it to a more desired size and shape, he or she exercises it hard. Hard working of the muscle creates a burn during part of the exercise set. The burn may be a sharp, hot feeling or it may be more of a deep ache. It may vary from slight to absolutely agonizing. This burn results from the build-up of lactic acid and perhaps other chemicals in the muscle tissue as by-products of the work performed. The muscle has been overloaded. This overload has caused some degree of structural alteration. Some destruction has taken place. It will require several hours, perhaps several days, for the muscle to reconstitute, to repair, to re-build. During this period of repair, there will probably be soreness in the muscle. This soreness may vary from slight and almost imperceptible to painful. It is currently believed that this "next day soreness" is the result of micro-tears in the muscle tissue. The "damaged" muscle tissue is repaired beyond its state prior to the "damage." So, the old structure was to some degree torn down in order that it could be rebuilt. It is a natural characteristic of the growth process that the product of restructuring is so constituted that it can handle the previous overload without being overloaded. In other words, the restructured muscle is stronger than the muscle which was destructured. And, to be stronger, it has been made bigger. Thus, the bodybuilder grows bigger, more shapely muscles. In the process of destructuring he or she creates the burn. In the destructured state, while restructuring is taking place, he or she experiences muscle soreness.

So, what Larry Scott was saying is that one of the secrets of bodybuilding is to work the muscles into the pain zone. It is the burn that is the biofeedback which tells the bodybuilder that he or she is stressing the muscle sufficiently. Although it is possible to stimulate muscle growth without creating a burn, the level and type of stress which stimulates maximal growth tends to create that sensation.

It is the bodybuilder, the seeker of large and shapely muscles, who is most interested in creating a burn. For the Olympic lifter and the powerlifter, the seekers of strength, the burn is of less interest. The low repetition workouts with heavy weights which the two latter lifters use for most of their training tend not to produce burns. But, even without burns there is discomfort and sometimes pain during a lift. The Olympic lifter and powerlifter become familiar with the discomfort and pain of straining with a hard lift.

All lifters know the pain of "next day soreness." If one has exercised hard enough to stimulate growth in size or strength of muscles, one will feel sore a few hours later. It is to this fact that Bill Pearl was alluding in my quote of him several paragraphs back.

And, so, the lifters' mantra — No pain, no gain.

The serious seeker of growth must be willing to endure the pain which is the by-product of her or his seeking. The challenge is to come to terms with the pain, to accept it, perhaps even to embrace it. An instructive example of this is offered by Raymond Coffin (1980) in his *Poetry for Crazy Cowboys and Zen Monks*.

Those not familiar with the training of a Zen monk probably envision a rather soft, perhaps even indulgent life. Scenes of serenity, such as quiet meditations and walks in gardens, breathtakingly beautiful in their simplicity, may come to mind. Through his poetry, Coffin describes scenes in stark contrast to these. He writes graphically of the o-sesshin, a seven day period of concentrated meditation. He tells of the strenuous effort and intense perseverance required to endure seven days with only three or four hours of sleep each night, and hour upon hour of meditation. The pain in the feet, knees, and waist build to the point that one thinks he is about to die. Usually, on the fourth day, Coffin relates, the monk stops running from his pain, accepting it as part of his personal experience. At this point the real work begins! Now, the monk begins to push.

In monasteries of the Renzai sect, there are about six o-sesshins each year. The most difficult is the one undertaken from the first to the seventh of December, a celebration of the enlightenment of Gautama (the Buddha). It is said that Gautama tried many severe disciplines, and not finding enlightenment through any of these, he sat under the bodhi-tree for seven days. On the morning of the eighth day he had his great awakening. During this celebration of the Rohatsu sesshin the Zen monk may sleep only two hours each night.

Beyond the o-sesshins, life in the monastery still can be difficult. "Excruciating experience" is the phrase chosen by Coffin to describe certain of the times. The most difficult year is the first, when the novice monk is on the bottom, working the hardest and sleeping the least. Coffin (1980, p. 10) remarks that, "...the ability of the body to adapt to adverse conditions is most amazing."

Is this not what lifting weights is all about? Lifting weights is a way of creating adverse conditions for the body to adapt to, in its most amazing way. Push it, strain it, stretch it, today, see its adaptation tomorrow.

And, oh, yes, your pain will confirm your success in creating an adverse condition.

I wanted to present the above perspective on life in the Zen monastery to show an example of the living of our mantra—No pain, no gain—in a context other than that of the world of iron. In addition, I wanted to show that this mantra applies in a highly spiritual discipline. Many examples could be enlisted from realms which appear much closer to the realm of weights. Going beyond these examples, I wanted to draw upon similarities between the disciplined path of lifting and the disciplined path of meditation, similarities of which the reader, by now, is aware.

Returning to the world of iron, one of the most personally revealing discussions of pain is that offered by Arnold Schwarzenegger (1977) in his autobiography. He tells us of his coming to terms with pain. Wanting to shock his muscles into growth, he and a training partner would take the weights out into the country and exercise one body part for hours. On one such outing, Schwarzenegger reports doing fifty-five sets of squats! His assessment is that his thighs had no chance to survive except to grow. It sounds like a truism when Schwarzenegger says that he and his partner experienced a lot of pain. That, he says, is the first time that he knew pain could become pleasure. In his own words, "It was a fantastic feeling to gain size from pain. All of a sudden I was looking forward to it as something pleasurable. ...I had just converted the pain into pleasure..." (Schwarzenegger, 1977, p. 85).

The key to this conversion of pain into pleasure is the shift in meaning. Pain, in and of itself is a strong sensation which demands attention. When it is perceived as meaning danger, that is, when fear is the emotional meaning attributed to it, it is very objectionable and something to be escaped. What I am calling attention to is the difference between sensation and perception. As pure **sensation**, pain is tolerable, even though unpleasant, throughout a considerable range of intensity. If it is **perceived** as having a desirable meaning, the range of tolerability can be broadened, and a mild to moderate level of pain, paradoxically, can even be experienced as pleasurable. This is based on the remarkable human ability to "make meaning" of sensations, thus creating perceptions. And, it is one's perceptions, the meaning one attributes to one's sensations, that is of importance. It is to one's perceptions that the person reacts or responds.

In an earlier chapter I discussed three body scripts and their corresponding personality styles. Each of the personality styles shows a particular attitude toward the pain encountered in weight training. Shifting to the sensation-perception distinction which I am making here, we can look at those personality styles again. For the lifter with a "disuse your body" script (the phobic personality style) the pains of training are perceived as danger signals. So, this lifter believes that he or she is hurting himself or herself when a muscle burn begins to develop. Likewise, next day muscle soreness is perceived as evidence that he or she "over did it." Such soreness is perceived as evidence that an injury has been incurred. So, this lifter reacts with some degree of fear whenever a muscle burn or muscle soreness arises. And thus, being phobic about these pains, this lifter undertrains. What is needed is a rather profound shift in perception.

For the lifter who has a "misuse your body" script the problem is just the opposite. The person of this impulsive personality style will tend either to ignore the pains of training, perceiving them as meaningless, or perceive them as signals to forge ahead without caution. The problem for this lifter is the failure to differentiate the growth pains (burns and next day soreness) from the pains of injury. So, he or she does not perceive the sharp pain in the elbow joint during a set of French curls as a warning to interrupt the set immediately. Nor does he or she perceive the persisting sharp pain in the lower back to indicate that a discontinuation of hyperextension sit ups is called for. Without perceiving the different meanings of burns and next day soreness on the one hand and the sharp pains and persistent aches on the other hand, this lifter is vulnerable to injury.

When a "use your body" script is operating (the self-actualizing personality style) the lifter is most likely to perceive pain correctly. He or she will tend to perceive sharp pains in the muscles or joints as danger signals to be heeded immediately. Perceived as such, this lifter would not be likely to continue the exercise, "working through the pain." Likewise, this lifter will tend to perceive muscle burns and next day soreness as valuable forms of biofeedback. This immediate feedback and delayed feedback are perceived as welcome guides in the design and execution of workout routines. It is this lifter who may make that perceptual shift, converting growing pains into pleasure.

For the dedicated lifter, the pains of muscle burns and next day soreness are the price of growth, a price that he or she is willing, perhaps even eager to pay. The payment, however, requires discipline. The pain of muscular growth may be taken as a metaphor for the pain of growth in other realms, as well. I suggest that you, the reader, extend this metaphor and see in your own life how your growth in other areas has fit the model of our mantra—No pain, no gain.

By definition, injury involves an overextension, an extending of limits beyond what the present structure can accommodate. As discussed in an earlier chapter and touched upon, again, in the present chapter, it is the lifter who has a "misuse your body" script who is psychologically most prone to injury. Having an impulsive style of living, this lifter is likely not to exercise reasonable caution.

Injuries are, of course, incurred by lifters who do not have an impulsive personality style. Injury is very democratic and does not discriminate against anyone who invites it. Lifters with a "disuse your body" script often show a quality of ineptness in their physical activities. This is easy to understand, since their body script has discouraged their full and varied participation in physical activities. Ironically, it is their phobic attitude which invites the very thing they are afraid of. This phenomenon is well known by coaches in many sports. It is sometimes stated as, "If you're afraid you'll get hurt, you will." It is the slight pause, that hesitation, that holding back which the phobic person does which invites injury. Consider the gymnast who slows down on her or his running approach to a hand spring, fearing the feat. The slight slowing down may be just enough to rob the gymnast of the momentum needed to carry her or his body through the full gyration and she or he lands on her or his surprised gluteus. The same principle applies to the phobic lifter. By not fully taking hold of the equipment and executing the movement with full commitment, an "accident" is invited. This is the lifter most likely to drop a plate on his foot, catch her or his finger in the weight stack, or get her hair in the chain of the Camstar.

So, what about the lifter with a "use your body" script? Even though neither impulsive nor phobic in personality style, this lifter, too, may incur injury. But with the self-actualizing personality style, the way of inviting injury is different. To be self-actualizing is to take reasonable risks. Working at or near one's growing edge is risky. In taking this risk there will sometimes be expansion far enough or frequent enough to exceed the growing edge, resulting in injury. I believe that honest errors of judgment can and do occur when one is trying to push one's body right up to the very edge of maximal growth. So, training injuries will be incurred even by the self-actualizing lifter. They will, however, be rare.

So injuries may be invited by an impulsive attitude, a phobic attitude, or by an honest error of judgment. With the phobic attitude, the lifter is overly cautious, paradoxically making herself or himself vulnerable to injury. In the case of the impulsive attitude, a **chronic state** of insufficient caution prevails. When the self-actualizing lifter makes a judgment leading to injury, the misjudgment has been an **instance** of insufficient caution.

It is apparent from the above discussion that most training injuries have a psychological root. One's body scripting, if it is of either the "disuse your body" or the "misuse your body" type, gives one a psychological set to invite an "accident." I place the word "accident" in quotes to acknowledge that even though these incidents may appear to "just happen," they are not truly accidental. The person who creates the incident may have no conscious intention of hurting herself or himself. In the case of the lifter with the "disuse your body" script and the resulting phobic style, he or she would in fact have the conscious intention of avoiding injury. Nevertheless, the scripting of these two types of lifters serves as a psychological predisposition for training injuries. People live out their psychological scripts even though they are not aware of them.

So far in discussing injury I have focused on training injuries. For the competitive lifter there is another activity in which he or she may incur injury. That, of course, is in the competition, itself. The lifting platform is a site of injury for many a lifter. The very essence of competition invites the lifter to exceed her or his previous limits, and the event encourages taking greater risks than in training. If one is ever going to take a big risk in lifting it is most likely to be while competing. It is this flirtation with danger that adds a thrill to the experience of competition for many lifters.

Before leaving the topic of injury and delving more fully into the meaning of competition, I want to introduce a final psychological source of injury. Sometimes people who have sustained an athletic injury, especially if it occurred in competition, are given special attention. The injured athlete may be only slightly less the hero than the victorious athlete. If one cannot be a champion, and hero-worshipping attention is strongly desired, injury could be the welcome route. Many an athlete has taken great pleasure in having admiring and sympathetic fans sign her or his cast. That could be a sweet enough temptation to allow one to be momentarily off balance or off in her or his timing, without any conscious intention whatsoever. I am not referring to the athlete who fakes injury for attention. Rather, I am positing that the benefit of admiring and sympathetic attention may at times serve as an unconscious motive to invite or allow an injury. The participation in injury can be an unconscious choice for the purpose of influencing or manipulating others.

Figure 9

The Relationship of Growth and Pain

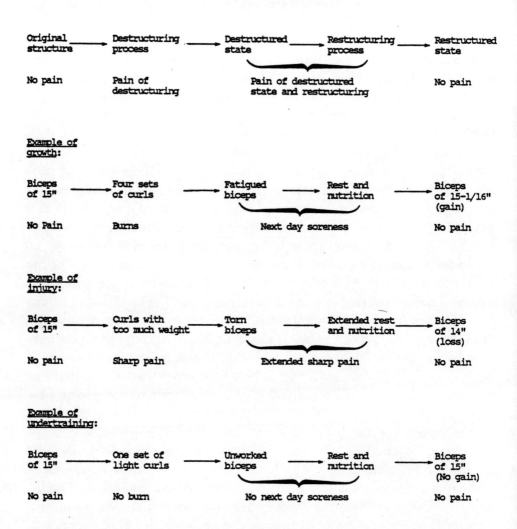

Original ——→ Destructuring ——→ Destructured ——→ Restructuring ——→ Restructured
structure   process   state   process   state

No pain   Pain of   Pain of destructured   No pain
                 destructuring   state and restructuring

Example of
growth:

Biceps ——→ Four sets ——→ Fatigued ——→ Rest and ——→ Biceps
of 15"   of curls   biceps   nutrition   of 15-1/16"
                                                             (gain)

No Pain   Burns   Next day soreness   No pain

Example of
injury:

Biceps ——→ Curls with ——→ Torn ——→ Extended rest ——→ Biceps
of 15"   too much weight   biceps   and nutrition   of 14"
                                                                 (loss)

No pain   Sharp pain   Extended sharp pain   No pain

Example of
undertraining:

Biceps ——→ One set of ——→ Unworked ——→ Rest and ——→ Biceps
of 15"   light curls   biceps   nutrition   of 15"
                                                             (No gain)

No pain   No burn   No next day soreness   No pain

Competition is "going public." This is true both for the bodybuilder and for the competitive lifter. In the case of the bodybuilder, training and competition are, of course, two entirely different things. The body-builder can train in the privacy of a home gym or in the less private arena of a public gym. As he or she trains, there may be onlookers. But what is seen is the training activity, the lifting and pumping, not the physique display, itself. Even if the bodybuilder does some posing in the gym, clearly this is practice posing, not the polished product which would be presented in a contest. In a real sense, the training and the practice posing are "private," or at least "semi-private." In the physique contest the bodybuilder "goes public." The event is advertised, and anyone with the price of admission can come in and see the show. In this competitive setting, the bodybuilder is making a public statement. He or she, by his or her very presence, is saying, "Here I am. Look at me. Judge me. Compare me to the others. Applaud me for the body I am, the body I have developed. Watch, and I will display my body, my self."

The situation is somewhat different for the competitive lifter. In her or his case, what is done in training and what is done in competition bear close resemblance, one to the other. The lifting which is done in competition is contained in the lifting which is done in training. The training, however, as is also the case with bodybuilding, may be done in the private arena of a home gym or the semi-private arena of a public gym. But, even in a public gym, most of the time one is not being watched closely. Although an actual lift or exercise can be seen, if anyone is interested, what that lift means in the context of one's training schedule is usually not known. It seems absurd to imagine a lifter announcing to the gym crowd, "Now I am going to do my fourth set of snatches. I'll be using seventy-five percent of my personal best, and going for five reps." Unless this is a recognized champion, offering an open training session for educational purposes, this lifter would be inviting a rash of rude and crude comments. Even on a day when the lifter is doing maximum lifts, the atmosphere is not one of sustained, let alone, rapt attention. Once again, it is in the context of the contest that the competitive lifter "goes public." The lifting meet is the public display of lifting prowess. When the competitor steps onto the lifting platform he or she is publicly stating, "Here I am. Watch me lift. Compare me to the other lifters. Applaud me for my demonstration of strength and skill."

Everyone is on her or his own in training. What one does in training is between the person and himself or herself, and, in some cases, between himself or herself and his or her trainer. Each person chooses to train as much or as little and in whatever manner he or she wishes. But, the physique or lifting contest is a publicly agreed upon event. Not only is the contest an open event, publicized and attended by all interested spectators who can afford a ticket, but it is a focal time for the competitors. They all agree to show up at the same place, at the same time, in order to show their best performances, under the same conditions. Everyone poses under the same light or lifts the same bar.

Just as there are archetypes, as I discussed in an earlier chapter, which are brought to life in the lifting activities, the "contest" is, itself, a lived archetype. The archetype of the contest is in evidence throughout history and across cultures. The contest is the pitting of a person against another person, animal, or mythical creature. It is the literal or symbolic entering into the "pit" to fight. From the Roman Colosseum to the YMCA gym the contest has been held over and over.

I believe that it is this participation in the bringing to life of the archetype of the contest which gives deep psychological meaning to lifting and physique competition. It is that going forth before the public, entering the "pit" to fight, symbolically, that draws people to the lifting platform and the posing dais. This participation offers a richness of experiencing. It offers one the opportunity to share in a central human experience which has been known since time immemorial. To strike a "double-biceps" in the pose off, or "lock out" a record breaking jerk on a fourth attempt, before a screaming crowd, brings one in touch with the same emotional experience that Samson must have had when he toppled the temple pillars. Whenever a man or a woman has tapped into that archetype of the contest, surely it has sent a wave of awe and excitement reverberating through his or her soul.

I am not saying that every time one enters a competition that it is a profound experience. What I am saying is that the contest archetype exercises a certain pull and offers the possibility of a psychologically deeply meaningful experience. The universality of the experience and the powerful emotion which is released when the archetype is tapped make the experience worthwhile.

All of us have in our collective unconscious the potential to recognize and experience the same profound feelings that the gladiators of all times and all places have felt. The battle has evolved to the level of the symbolic in its manifestation in the weight sports. In physique contests it is the "look" of victorious power which is contested. And, in competitive lifting, it is the demonstration of great strength, as symbol of supremacy, which is at stake. In both cases, the symbol of physically overcoming the competitor is contested, not a literal fight. It is to our credit to have humanized the contest in this way, and not to request a literal maiming or killing to prove the physical superiority of one modern gladiator over another. (The contest is, obviously, much closer to the literal in boxing and full-contact karate.)

Just as the form of the contest in the weight sports evidences a humanized evolution, substituting symbolic victory of muscle over muscle for the literal victory by maiming or killing, there is room for still more evolution of attitude toward competition. Even in the civilized competition of the weight world, the predominant attitude is that there are winners and losers. In the technical language of game theory, this outlook corresponds to the playing of a "zero-sum game." In a zero-sum game the loss of one player equals the gain of another. So, if you add the losses and the gains, the sum is zero. There are some limitations or even problems inherent in the zero-sum game outlook. First of all, when a contest is so defined, for there to be a winner, there must be a loser. And, no one wants to be a loser. The way contests are usually arranged, a first place is awarded to the winner, and depending on the number of competitors, second, third, or even fourth place may be awarded. But there is, by definition, only one winner, one first place. Everyone else is a loser. Some are "more losers" than others, but everyone who doesn't walk away with a trophy inscribed with "First" is a loser. The upshot of this is that many people emerge from a contest feeling bad about themselves.

The zero-sum game encourages a chauvinistic attitude, rather than an attitude of equality and peership. This may be more or less subtle in its effect. But, when a winner is defined vis-a-vis a loser, the tendency is to praise and identify with the winner and to degrade the loser. The honor and loyalty of team members and fans in the pursuit of being winners creates definite lines of strain. This is, then, another negative effect of competition. Even if competition affords an opportunity to learn and practice cooperation within one's team, it discourages a spirit of cooperation between members of one team and the other. In addition, as the team gets smaller and smaller, there is cooperation with fewer and fewer others, until, in the case of the individual competitor, all cooperation is in violation of the rules of the zero-sum game.

In entering the iron world as a path for personal growth one would be at cross purposes to become heavily invested in winning. Winning not only is not everything, it may be nothing in comparison to the things which can be learned in the process of lifting and competing.

What I am suggesting is the use of competition as a "nonzero-sum game." Rather than defining the participants as winners and losers, everyone can emerge a winner. This would eliminate the bad feelings and erosion of self-esteem which attend being declared a loser. It would also allow for more experience of peership and cooperation. We have evolved, as I said earlier, to the point that the muscle to muscle contest is symbolic. It is no longer a fight to maim or kill. So, can we also evolve beyond the point of inflicting psychic pain and discouraging cooperative relationships?

How, then, can the lifter who has chosen to pursue lifting as a path of growth benefit from competition? How can lifting and physique competition be approached as a nonzero-sum game? These become important questions when the value of competition as an opportunity to declare oneself publicly and to participate in the living out of the contest archetype is realized.

First, one can shift the emphasis from comparing oneself to the others, to measuring one's growth against one's potential. The lifting or physique contest can be the occasion for marking one's progress. How well am I doing, relative to the previous meet? How well am I doing, relative to my practice sessions? In a sense, then, the contest is with oneself. What the other competitors do is, really, irrelevant. What I am focusing on is how I am doing, relative to what I am capable of doing.

Second, and more profound in its effect, is the shift of focus from outcome to process. This means to place the value on the process of competing rather than on the score. It means to really enter into the lifting or the posing without concern for how one places. In oriental philosophy this is called "detachment." Competing with detached interest means that one has let go of judging how one is doing, relative to the other competitors, or even how one is doing relative to oneself! The competition is no longer dead serious. What is important is enjoying oneself as one explores oneself through the process of lifting or posing. The meaning is found in the journey, not in the arrival at the destination.

In terms of exploring oneself, and beyond that, working on oneself, competition offers something different for lifters having each of the three types of body script. For the lifter with a "disuse your body" script, a central issue is her or his phobic attitude. Such a person tends to be shy and overly cautious. The lifting or physique contest is an excellent opportunity for the exploration of shyness and cautiousness. By putting oneself in the contest situation the lifter can explore, in depth, her or his thoughts and emotions. He or she can come face to face with the enemy — fear. By being willing to face this fear, feel it fully, and act in spite of it, the lifter is working on personal growth. It is this acting in spite of the experience of fear that erodes the phobic attitude. The contest is a place for this lifter to practice taking the risk of going all out, of making that total commitment in each lift or each pose. By making that committed effort, without hesitating and without holding back, this lifter can learn that whatever happens is almost never as bad as he or she had feared. And, in fact, what happens is usually far, far better than the phobic attitude would predict. With practice, the previously shy lifter can come to lift or pose boldly and enjoy the process, free from phobic feelings. The key is the consistent working on oneself.

For the lifter of impulsive attitude, the issue which can be worked on in a contest is the opposite. As we have seen, with this "misuse your body" script there is a tendency not to be cautious enough. So the lifting or physique contest is an opportunity to experiment with holding back a bit. This lifter can experience what it is like for her or him to proceed with some caution. So, instead of calling for a weight which is far more than he or she has lifted, this lifter could call for a weight lifted in practice or slightly more. If this is the lifter's opening lift, he or she could call for a weight which is less than his or her best, a weight that he or she can easily lift. In the case of posing, this process of experimenting may be more subtle. He or she may stick with the poses and sequence practiced, not attempting anything on impulse. The idea is to "break the script" by not acting on impulse and thereby decreasing the probability of injury, in the case of the competitive lifter. For the physique contestant the risk of injury during her or his posing is slight. The "misusing" of her or his body will take place in training. Even so, the practice of caution in the meet is worthwhile. First of all, it can carry over into training. Second, and perhaps of more potency in its effect, the exercise of caution may bring the person face to face with his or her urge to be impulsive. The thoughts and feelings surrounding this can then be explored for deeper personal understanding.

The self-actualizing lifter, lifting from a "use your body" script, can use the contest as an arena for exploring that middle ground of being neither too cautious, nor not cautious enough, being neither shy and timid, nor impulsive. He or she can also explore the de-emphasizing of "serious competition" with others. This can be developed to the extent of learning about detachment from outcome. This lifter can raise her or his consciousness by coming to that point of enjoying the process of competing without the negative effects of being overly attached to the results. He or she can enjoy the experience of living out the archetype of the contest, hampered not by timidity, shyness, or over attachment to the outcome. And, every contestant who does this is a clear winner.

Chapter 7

ANSWERING THE CRITICS

I WONDER IF any other sports have been as misunderstood and as criticized as the weight sports. Perhaps so. Maybe it is because of my involvement in the iron world that I have been more attuned to hearing these criticisms. And, if I had spent as much time involved with some other sports, maybe I would then have had my interest in them challenged, too. What I do know is that I have heard a great deal of criticism about the iron game and have been personally criticized for my involvement in it. I don't recall having had people challenge my interest in judo, karate, or aikido, when I was participating in each of those martial arts. And, I don't get challenged for my ongoing practice of Hatha Yoga or t'ai ch'i chuan, although these are not considered sports.

I believe that the bulk of the criticism of lifting is based on misunderstanding, often coupled with a feeling of personal threat. With respect to the phenomena of lifting, ignorance abounds. Most people are not well-informed as to the biomechanics, exercise physiology, and nutritional aspects of lifting weights, let alone the psychological aspects. And even the events themselves, posing, Olympic lifting and powerlifting, are often not well understood outside the circle of participants and avid fans. This continues to be the case today, even though more and more people have been exposed to lifting over the past years. But ignorance, by itself does not explain the strong negative reactions which some people show. This, I see, as evidence that something about lifting is experienced as a personal threat. In addition to these sources of criticism, there are also some legitimate criticisms which can be levied against the lifting activities and the lifters. I want to address each of these three areas, one by one.

First, let us look at the legitimate criticisms. Any lifter, no matter how much he or she loves the world of iron, would surely admit, if honest, that it contains a lot of "hype." In fact, I don't know of any sport which has as much hype as lifting weights. True, professional wrestling has more, but long ago it went beyond any reasonable limit for being considered a sport and into the realm of staged entertainment.

In the weight world the hype comes from the promoters, the equipment manufacturers, the distributors of nutritional supplements and ergogenic aids, and the professional instructors. Promoters, in their enthusiasm to sell tickets sometimes advertise their contests in ways that are gaudy and overstated. This is more often the case with physique shows where there is a potential for large crowds. The titles awarded are sometimes ridiculously grandiose, with the trophies reflecting this grandiosity. There is something absurd about seeing a man or a woman standing on stage receiving a trophy which is far taller than he or she. I have seen entry forms for physique shows where considerable space is devoted to descriptions of how big and outstandingly "beautiful" the trophies are! The overdone quality of some contests — grandiose titles with trophies to match — certainly cheapens the sport. Paradoxically, many promoters put on poorly run shows. I have witnessed regional and even national physique contests where lighting was poor, public address systems have cut out, the master of ceremonies was not well spoken (using poor grammar, not speaking clearly, getting cue cards out of order), and, in one case, a contestant was left standing on stage, befuddled, as the sound system poured out strains of someone else's posing tape! These sorts of things occur with much too great regularity. These two phenomena — contest hype and shabbily run contests — certainly do not invite the respect and serious interest from the public. Promoters are also apparently sometimes lax in setting the ground rules and explaining the procedures to contestants. Several times, for instance, I have seen contestants awkwardly wander about the stage following their posing routine, not knowing where to exit. Worse, still, I have witnessed rude and unsportsman like behavior on stage. This occurred in a major contest where I had taken a woman friend to introduce her to the physique contest. During a "pose down," with six or eight men on stage, two of the men began elbowing each other and trying to push each other out of the way. The hip and shoulder pushing and deliberate stepping in front of each other became the most prominent activity on stage, and continued for several minutes. This was one of the strongest images which my friend took away with her. Adequate briefing of contestants could forbid such displays.

Equipment manufacturers sometimes make claims which cannot be backed up with actual results. When a manufacturer makes a public claim that certain growth in size or strength will result from using its apparatus, and people do not find their progress to match the claim, they are, understandably, disappointed. Often the claim is an implied one, one which meets the letter of the law in terms of fair advertising, but not the spirit of the law. Just consider for a moment your own reaction if in reading a lifting magazine you come across three or four advertisements each claiming that its equipment will outperform all others, producing unrivaled results. Credibility, of course, slips. Certainly, many equipment manufacturers are honest and tasteful in their advertising. There are those, however, who propagate pure hype.

Even more blatant in overstating the value of their products are some of the distributors of nutritional supplements and ergogenic aids. Some of these products are not backed by scientific evidence of their effectiveness. Unashamedly, some distributors go right ahead claiming that their product is an incredibly effective muscle builder. Such activities are not limited to the fly-by-night purveyors of snake oil, but are sometimes engaged in by the well-established companies. A few months ago I received in the mail a letter which indicated that one of the major companies was having its wrists slapped by the Federal Trade Commission. The letter started out as follows:

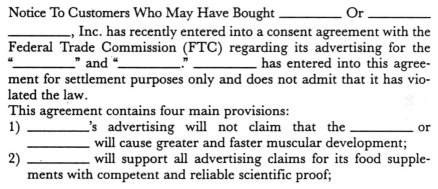

Notice To Customers Who May Have Bought _____ Or _____
_____, Inc. has recently entered into a consent agreement with the Federal Trade Commission (FTC) regarding its advertising for the "_____" and "_____." _____ has entered into this agreement for settlement purposes only and does not admit that it has violated the law.
This agreement contains four main provisions:
1) _____'s advertising will not claim that the _____ or _____ will cause greater and faster muscular development;
2) _____ will support all advertising claims for its food supplements with competent and reliable scientific proof;

Someone in the company became overly zealous and went the way of the snake oil salesman. My guess is that this caused a great deal of embarrassment, as well as a great deal of financial loss through purchase refunds, to the members of this large company. This sort of thing, again, can decrease the credibility of the distributors and reflect badly on the world of iron.

Professional instructors, too, have added their share of hype. Some have placed advertisements in magazines which contained explicit or implied promises of results which anyone who is knowledgeable of lifting would readily recognize as overstatements, at best. The hype is not limited to the less honest professionals of the mail order training courses. It is rampant among many of the so-called "instructors" in the gym chains. I have known some very good instructors who worked in the clubs, but for the most part, my experience has been that the majority of health club instructors did not know a French curl from a Zottman curl, let alone the purpose of each. Too often, these instructors are not well trained. So, they give honest seekers of muscle misinformation, leading to poor training and less than optimal gains. If they also are expected to sell club memberships, they may be prone to making up stories in order to sell the customers.

Several years ago I took a friend with me to the gym where I was then training. It was a moderately well equipped club, a unit of a major national chain. Purportedly for safety's sake, it was required that all visitors to the club had to be taken through their workouts with a one-on-one instructor. So, I went about my workout, naively leaving my friend in the hands of the instructor. Perhaps a half-hour later, I turned to see my friend passed out on the floor, with the instructor nervously scurrying about for help. My friend's introduction to weight training had consisted of multiple super-sets of squats on a Smith machine and inclined dumbbell presses! Needless to say, he never asked to go back to the gym with me.

The point that I am making is that there are a number of legitimate criticisms which can be made against various aspects of the iron game. Certain promoters, equipment manufacturers, distributors of supplements, and instructors, themselves, engage in practices which put the weight sports in a bad light. And, although similar criticisms can justifiably be made against other sports, as well, I believe that there are more legitimate criticisms of the iron game than is true for most other sports.

What is more interesting to me, however, are the illegitimate criticisms. The legitimate criticisms seem rather obvious. The criticisms which stem from misunderstandings of what lifting is about, however, have some subtleties. I want to explore several of these criticisms and suggest some of the misunderstandings which give rise to them.

Since weightlifting, both Olympic style weightlifting and powerlifting, have been minor sports, they are not as well understood by the public as are the major sports. This is simply a result of their limited exposure. The exposure of these lifting sports which is given is often not very representative. If, for instance, a network sports program gives a few minutes to a weightlifting event, the choice is usually to show the super-heavyweights. Much more time has been given to the heavier weights than to the lighter weight classes. The result is that many people with this limited exposure believe that competent weightlifters are big, heavy, and rotund. They infer, then, that the lifters are somewhat slow and ponderous. The negative attitude which I have heard expressed is, "Who would want to look like that?" The inference is that if one lifts weights, one will come to look like that. It is amazing how ingrained that equation is — lifting weights equals big, bulky, rotund. I remember a conversation shortly after winning a state Olympic lifting title in the 123 pound class as a high school student. The boss at my summer job found me writing a training schedule during a work break and asked me what it was. When I told him what I was doing and that I lifted weights, he asked, curiously, "Why don't you have big muscles." To him, a weight-lifter was a huge man with very large, bulging muscles. The probability is that the only picture of a weightlifter which he had ever seen was that of Paul Anderson.

In the mass media coverage of bodybuilding, there is further promotion of the image that lifters are huge. This comes from the fact that the most coverage is of the biggest events, in which world class bodybuilders are the ones seen.

So, because of limited exposure to the weight sports, the general public has the biased view that men who lift weights are huge. They are either developed to the point that the uninitiated viewer would likely see as grotesque, or they are the rotund shape of most super-heavyweights. The media want to show the most spectacular lifters, and by so doing, create the impression that this is what all lifters must look like. If the person doesn't relate to those two kinds of bodies, then he may well stay away from the weights, and criticize the weight sports as making people look ugly. The obvious fallacy is that these bodies are not the automatic and uniform result of lifting weights. First of all, most of these bodies have been developed over many years of highly specialized, high intensity training. Second, there is a certain genetic make-up which is required for the attainment of the muscular size and shape of the world class bodybuilder or the over-all size and strength of the world class super-heavyweight weightlifter. Just anyone can not attain that size, strength, and development even if he dearly wants to! It is not generally understood that a genetic potential, plus years of specialized training are both required.

There is another issue, closely related to the one just discussed. There is sometimes a cult-like quality that emerges among groups of lifters. Within the cult there can come to be a shared esthetic, which may be quite different from the more widely held esthetic. Consider this simple explanation. If a group of people are accustomed to seeing thirteen-inch arms on men, and someone develops a muscular sixteen-inch arm, he may be admired for his accomplishment. If, however, a man comes along with a muscular arm of twenty-inches, he is more likely to be seen as a freak than a man to be admired. The men with thirteen-inch arms may think better than to call him a freak to his face, but they will probably discuss this among themselves. And, if our man with the twenty-inch arms tells them that he developed these arms by lifting weights, the oversimplified reaction is to criticize the lifting of weights. Lifting is then identified as the process for becoming grotesque. For another group of men, who have all developed sixteen-inch arms, the eighteen-inch arm may be held out as a worthy achievement. As soon as the eighteen-inch arm has become a common enough sight within that clique, the twenty-inch arm which was repulsive to the men in general (who had thirteen-inch arms), may be a thing of true beauty.

I remember reading an interview with a Mr. Olympia one time in which he stated that he wanted arms so big that "the average man on the street would vomit" when he saw them. Implicit in this Mr. Olympia's statement is the recognition that what would be revered within the "cult" would be disgusting to those outside the cult.

The psychological principle involved in this is known as the "adaptation level." Basically, what this principle means is that perception is based in part on what one is accustomed to perceiving. That is, as one perceives a certain level of something over and over, he or she gets used to that level. This is the level to which one becomes adapted. The perception of a new stimulus is then influenced by that level to which one has become adapted. So, if one is used to seeing thirteen-inch arms, one adapts to that level and notices contrasts to that. The sixteen-inch arm would seem big. The twenty-inch arm would be so far beyond the adaptation level that one's perceptual reaction would be strong.

The adaptation level with respect to the visual perception of physique is very different for those in the iron world and those not in that world. The clear implication is that the world of iron would often be misunderstood by those outside it.

There is an old erroneous belief about lifting weights which is clearly founded on ignorance. This is the belief that lifting weights can or will make one "muscle bound." Although I do not hear this criticism as often as I used to, many people seem still to hold this belief. I remember being asked once by someone who just learned that I was a lifter, "But, aren't you afraid that you'll get muscle bound?" Another time, when I was in graduate school, my roommate invited one of his clinical supervisors to a party at our apartment. This psychologist had been a high school basketball coach in his earlier days, before getting a doctorate in clinical psychology. When he saw my weightlifting trophies on the fireplace mantel, he expressed his opinion that it was good that I was physically active, but that he really didn't know if he approved of lifting weights as a form of exercise. What he was implying was that I was in danger of becoming muscle bound.

My guess is that the myth of muscle bound weightlifters arose from some limited observations of a few lifters who were tight, stiff, and perhaps moved slowly. This condition of limited flexibility could arise, of course, from improper training. A lack of stretching and an exclusive use of only partial excursions in exercises would lead to limited flexibility. But this is not the result of lifting weights *per se*. It is the result of what one has **not** done. That is, it is the result of not stretching and of not working the muscles through a full range of motion (full extension to full contraction).

Another factor which may have reinforced the belief that lifting weights leads to a muscle bound condition is the sensation that one feels when a muscle is pumped. A muscle, pumped to full turgidity feels tight, and the skin surrounding it may feel stretched, adding to the tight feeling. But, this is a temporary condition, lasting only a few minutes. I sometimes check my pump when I am doing triceps work by putting my arms in the double biceps pose position, but without flexing my biceps. Ordinarily, the tips of my relaxed fingers just graze my anterior deltoids. When my triceps are well pumped, however, my finger tips are far above my anterior deltoids, even with my arms well relaxed. For a few minutes I have a decreased triceps flexibility. As soon as the excess blood is invited elsewhere, this transient "muscle boundedness" is over.

Informed opinion, now, is that the proper use of weights will not make one muscle bound. In fact, research has shown that lifting weights through a full range of motion can increase flexibility. This fact, together with the knowledge that progressive resistance training is the most efficient means of increased muscle strength, has led trainers in almost all sports to include weights at least in off season training. Especially impressive is that trainers of swimmers and basketball players now commonly include progressive resistance exercise in their programs.

I remember the shock that came several years back when it was revealed that the University of Iowa basketball team were lifting weights. The result was a significant increase in jumping height for the players, with no loss of speed or coordination.

I want to make one final point about the use of progressive resistance training in the non-weight sports. It seems so obvious, and yet this point is sometimes missed. The point is, lifting weights is not a substitute for skills practice in a particular non-weight sport. Obviously, lifting weights will not improve a basketball player's shooting accuracy. So, if on season training time is devoted to lifting weights at the expense of skills practice, the players will become poorer players as they become stronger. It would be incorrect, however, to say that lifting weights makes for poorer players. Lack of skills practice makes for poorer players. But, if off season weight training leads to players who are stronger and can jump higher, then these factors added to skills well-honed on season means a well improved team. Training, as strengthening and conditioning, needs to be distinguished from skills building.

Now, back to hardcore lifting. Perhaps the most convincing evidence, and certainly the most graphic evidence that lifting weights does not make one muscle bound is the incredible flexibility which many accomplished lifters demonstrate. John Grimek is famous for his demonstrations of isolated muscle control and extreme flexibility. And, he is an Olympic lifting champion, representing the USA in the 1936 Olympic Games, a Mr. America, Mr. U.S.A., and Mr. Universe. This man, epitome of the weightlifting champion, could twist and bend like a yogi. And, outstanding, as John Grimek is, he is but one example. The public is often surprised, if not shocked to see how flexible a well trained weightlifter can be. So, let us put to rest that misinformed opinion that gives rise to the criticism that lifting weights is dangerous because it will make one muscle bound.

In the past few years a new criticism of weight training has emerged. As jogging became extremely popular and cardiovascular conditioning came into the consciousness of millions of people, weight training began to be criticized for not being a good provider of this. This criticism really misses the point. Even a rudimentary understanding of physiological specificity reduces this criticism into a whisper of "so what?" Lifting weights builds muscle size and strength. And, it does so more efficiently and more completely than any other activity. This is its focus, its physical purpose. Recall, that in an earlier chapter I discussed the parameters of physical activity: strength, speed, flexibility, endurance, and coordination. To develop each of these, one needs to engage in an activity which emphasizes the respective parameters. Any given activity will emphasize a particular one or combination of these. No single activity develops all of these maximally.

Weight training focuses on strength building, with speed, flexibility, endurance, and coordination taking a second priority, or less, depending on the specific type of strength training which one does. For this reason, a well trained lifter stretches for flexibility and does some aerobic work such as running, power walking, swimming, or bicycling for cardiovascular conditioning.

Research has shown that lifting weights can be done in such a manner that it provides good cardiovascular conditioning. To do so, one must lift in an aerobic manner. This means to keep active and thereby keep one's pulse in the "training zone" for a minimum of twelve to twenty minutes. One can do this with "circuit training," moving immediately from one set of an exercise to one set of the next exercise, and so on, without resting between the sets. When the circuit of exercise stations is complete, it can be repeated as many times as necessary to provide the number of sets or the amount of exercise time desired. When this training method is followed, an aerobic advantage is gained, but at a loss of maximal muscle building. Even when high intensity lifting is being used, perhaps with super-sets or tri-sets for good muscle burns and big pumps, some rest is required between one super-set and the next or one tri-set and the next. Otherwise, cardiovascular condition sets the limit on the exercise intensity rather than muscle fatigue. Similarly, in Olympic or powerlifting training rests are taken between sets so that maximal muscular output is reached, rather than a cardiovascular limit.

My point is that it is more appropriate to appreciate weight training for what it is, than to criticize it for what it is not.

"Okay," continues the critic, "so lifting weights is the best way to develop big, strong muscles. But, those big muscles are useless." To say that big muscles are useless is, I believe, to reveal one's misunderstanding of the meaning of weight training. Earlier material in the present book has expanded on the meaning of lifting. On the most surface level, the development of a strong, muscled body opens more possibilities. There is much more that a person of strong body can do. First of all, overall bodily strength is a protection against injury as one does whatever one does in the world. Minor bumps, falls, twists, pulls, and strains are inevitable as one moves through the world. A strong body is able to withstand more of these physical insults than is a weak body. Beyond this protection against injury, having a strong body means that one can do more. It means that one can accomplish tasks which are not possible for someone with a weaker body. The stronger person can rearrange the furniture more easily, carry her or his bags at the airport more easily, and open the new jar of peanut butter more easily. In all forms of physical recreation, other things being equal, the stronger the person, the better he or she will do. In general, then, getting stronger means becoming physically more able. And this can contribute to a sense of competence in living.

On a deeper psychological level, too, the development of a strong, muscled body allows more possibilities. A stronger body opens the potential of pushing beyond the ordinary physical limits and exploring more of the realm of the possible human. Exceeding the ordinary introduces one to the wonders of the extraordinary. Much of the present book is, itself, a discourse on the vast opportunity for personal growth through the development and use of muscle.

Two more of the criticisms of weight lifters which are heard from time to time are based on grossly naive generalizations. The criticisms are that lifters are narcissistic and that they are dumb. With respect to the first of these, I doubt that lifters as a group are any more self-centered than are other athletes as a group. This criticism probably has its origin in some people's limited exposure to the viewing of posing. It could be a quick conclusion to draw, seeing someone posing in front of a mirror, that this is an extreme narcissist. Certainly, there are many self-centered bodybuilders. The point is, however, that there are many egotists in other sports as well (and many egotists who do not even partake of sports). The following equation, Bodybuilder = Narcissist, is not true. Not only are not all narcissists bodybuilders, but all bodybuilders are not narcissists. Every sport has its narcissists. This criticism of bodybuilders is naive not only in its gross generalization, but in its failure to differentiate between egotism (a pathological condition) and the healthy urge for self-actualization. The striving to realize one's potential is a natural urge.

The second naive generalization is that weightlifters are dumb. I have heard this further generalized to "athletes are dumb." We can speculate about the origins of this prejudice. I had an experience, however, which gave me an insight as to how this belief may be propagated. In my first Olympic style contest someone approached me, after my final lift, to congratulate me. I had just tripled my body weight, and more, in my three lift total. I was feeling excited and still experiencing an adrenaline rush. As I spoke in response to this fan I was mildly shocked to hear myself. I was barely articulate! A few minutes later I was back to what felt like a normal state, and I was again well spoken. I experienced a similar thing at another contest while I was in college, a year or two later. I had no way to explain why I had sounded like a blithering idiot, but I remembered the experiences vividly.

I now have an explanation. I believe that two factors were at work to render me to a state of babbling. First, I was "overcharged" with energy. A heavy energy charge calls for expression through the gross musculature. A high charge of energy overloads the systems of finely coordinated muscle action. So, just as I could not have executed a watch repair at that time, even if I had had the skill, I could not coordinate the intricate set of speech muscles very well. Thus, my slurred and stammering speech. But, beyond this, the content of my speech was not clear. Not only did I have a diction problem, but I had a problem expressing an idea in a grammatical way. I now believe that the reason for this was that my consciousness was predominantly of my right cerebral hemisphere. Speaking, both understanding of speech and production of speech, is a left cerebral hemisphere function. What happened, I believe, is that my left brain was not fully operating. Thus, I spoke as if lacking in the fundamentals of education.

What frequently happens is that athletes are interviewed, publicly, either during or immediately following their performance, and therefore are not at their left brain best. (Remember, as discussed in the chapter on the Apollonian and Dionysian orientations, the left lobe processes data by sequential analysis of abstract, symbolic "bits." This involves a logical, temporal, cause and effect approach. The right lobe processes data in a holistic, integrative way, providing recognition of patterns. It may be primarily involved in imagery and emotional expression.) While performing, athletically, much of one's consciousness is that of the right lobe. One has an overall, integrated body sense, while recognizing and producing certain patterns of body movement. There may be mental imagery accompanying the bodily activity. And, most often, emotion is running high. The interview is a request to shift rather rapidly from a right lobe consciousness to a left lobe consciousness. Not making such a shift rapidly enough results in the interviewee making some less than profound statements, and absolutely inane utterances. Thus, the listener can be led to conclude, "This guy is dumb!" It is too much to ask Dionysus, at the height of his ecstasy, to give the reasoned, measured oration of Apollo.

If these criticisms were not enough, our critic can utter one more, specific to bodybuilding. The final criticism is that, "Bodybuilding is not a sport." Recognizing the distinction which is sometimes drawn between "sports" and "athletics," this critic might concede that "Bodybuilding is a sport, but it is not an athletic event." (The distinction here is between the broader category, "sports," meaning pleasant pastimes or diversions, and the sub-category of sports which is athletics, meaning those sports which involve competition requiring strength and endurance. By this distinction, automobile racing, billiards, fishing, and trap shooting are sports, but not athletics.)

This criticism is based, I believe, on ignorance of what constitutes the bodybuilding enterprise. If one sees only the posing, and regards it as the same as the "swimsuit competition" of the Miss America pageant, then, I agree, it would not be an athletic endeavor. Bodybuilding is unusual in that it is constituted of two distinct activities — lifting and posing. Surely, no one would argue that lifting weights is not an athletic endeavor. If there were any doubt, the skeptic would need only to experience a typical training session of a hardcore bodybuilder in order to be convinced. The posing activity, taken in isolation from the lifting, is the target of the claim that bodybuilding is not an athletic event. There are clearly three errors involved in that claim. First, the posing is for the display of the product of the lifting. The posing cannot be isolated from the lifting activity, for it is the results of lifting, that is, the weightlifting-developed body that is being shown. Second, posing is itself an arduous task. This is a fact which is often not realized by those who have not done it. It may look easy, but posing for several minutes requires strength and endurance, in addition to coordination, balance, and muscle control. Let the uninitiated try to follow any bodybuilder of even state or regional class stature through her or his posing routine and the physical skills and demands will be apparent. And, third, when posing ability is itself a factor being judged, this is in essence no different from judging the esthetics of high diving, figure skating, or the floor routine of gymnastics. I believe that these three factors clearly qualify the physique contest as an athletic event. Add to this the athletic training for the event, and bodybuilding is certainly an athletic event, as well as a sport.

These, then, are the several criticisms of lifting weights which I have heard over the years, based, on a lack of information or on misinformation. And, these are my responses to those criticisms.

Near the beginning of the present chapter, I mentioned that ignorance of the iron sports does not explain the strong negative reactions sometimes levied against them. The legitimate criticisms and criticisms based on lack of knowledge constitute the content of the negative opinions. Another factor must be present, however, to account for the vehemence of some critics. Such a strong negative reaction implies that there is some underlying psychological issue. One does not get emotional over issues which are not personally relevant, psychologically speaking. It is to this factor I now turn.

Early in my lifting career I had a couple of experiences which gave me a glimpse of the psychological factor behind criticizing the lifting sports. One Saturday, when I was a freshman in college, I invited a friend to go work out with me at the YMCA where I was training. Having lifted some in high school, and being no stranger to the weights, he accepted, and asked to bring along a couple of his other friends. One of his friends seemed a bit nervous as we commenced to lift. He paced about and talked a lot, mostly of things unrelated to the activity at hand. Then, I noticed that he kept looking at my arms, and then at his. At one point after I had finished using a bar, he proceeded to lift it overhead, as I had done, only to have one of the fifty pound plates slide off the bar. Of course, the second fifty left the other side of the bar a brief moment later. He uttered some justification for his failure to lift the barbell, and left the weight room. My conclusion was that he was probably jealous of me and embarrassed as he compared his arms and his lifting to mine. After that day, he was never very friendly. Interestingly, he devoted a great deal of time and money to the "souping up" of his car that year. Perhaps the four speed manual transmission with which he replaced his stock automatic gave him some compensation for his seeing his arms as small.

The next incident occurred a couple years later after I transferred to a private university. I was living in a dormitory with a roommate. One of his friends had dropped by and the two of them were just hanging out and talking. I was packing my gym bag, getting ready to go work out. When my roommate's friend saw me, he asked what I was going to do. Naively, I said I was going to lift weights. He responded with a condescending look and tone of voice, saying, "I pity people like you." I was taken aback! His previously friendly way of relating was totally changed. I don't remember what more he said, only that he elaborated on his pity for people who lift weights. I did not offer an argument, but noticed how very thin he was. I went on to my workout, thinking on my way that he, being so thin, must be threatened by the reminder of others' robustness.

What these two occurrences suggested to me was that boys or young men who are self-conscious about their own physical image may be threatened by someone whom they see as somehow more physically developed. Or, put simply, they are jealous of those who are bigger, or stronger, or more developed. Interestingly, in these cases, both young men were considerably taller than I. The difference between us was that I was more muscular.

In these two incidents I learned of the psychological factor underlying the criticizing of the weight sports. At the time I called it jealousy. Now, I can elaborate on that explanation.

Lifting weights calls attention to, and leads to an exaggeration of the masculine. First, in the act of lifting, be it training or competition, one calls attention to one's strength, to one's muscles in action. Second, in posing one is making an ostentatious display of one's muscles. And, it is big, strong muscles which are a primary symbol and expression of masculinity. The development of muscle is one of the recognized secondary sexual characteristics of the human male. (In development of the male, the male genitalia are the primary sexual characteristic; secondary sexual characteristics include a deeper voice, more body hair, more facial hair, and greater muscular development, relative to the female.)

What I am saying, then, is that **since lifting weights exaggerates the masculine, it can threaten those who have a weak sense of their own masculinity.** So, for the person who wants to feel masculine, but has a weak masculine image, the whole iron world can be an unpleasant reminder of his inadequacy. It is this threat to one's feeling of self-esteem which can motivate one, consciously or unconsciously, to be critical of the world of iron. This motivation provides the energy for vehement criticism, while the several items based on limited information or misinformation which I have discussed earlier in this chapter provide the content. Further content is offered for legitimate criticism, as was also discussed. But, whether the content of criticism is legitimate or not, it is the vehemence of the criticism which reflects the felt threat.

This exaggeration of the masculine in the iron world creates an interesting situation for the participation of women. The most common criticism of women in lifting is that "they aren't feminine." Some people may find a woman who develops her animus or masculine side attractive, and other people may not. So, there is room for expression of esthetic preference. But, again, a vehement criticism bespeaks a criticism born of personal threat. We can add, then, a corollary to the statement above, namely, **since lifting weights exaggerates the masculine side of a woman lifter, it can be a tremendous threat to men who have a weak sense of their own masculinity.** Imagine how a man who wants to feel masculine, but who has a weak masculine image, would feel watching a woman lift more than he could, or seeing a woman flex a set of biceps larger than his. I believe it takes a man who is quite sure of his own masculinity to be able really to appreciate and support women Olympic style lifters, powerlifters, and bodybuilders. And, of course, there are surely women who, themselves not having developed their masculine side, may be jealous of their sisters who have.

There are those who recognize the legitimate criticisms of the world of iron. And, there are those who, out of ignorance, are soft spoken critics. Then, there are the vehement critics, threatened to the core of their self image by what they see. It is some of those in the third category who may go beyond mere criticism to actually try to discourage or stop others from pursuing an interest in lifting. Those who take this actively oppositional stance are those who are, in the term of Wilhelm Reich (1949), "emotionally plagued."

By the term "emotional plague," Reich was referring to the behavior of discouraging or stopping other people's aliveness. It is a chronic opposition to the healthy expression of life energy in others. Reich stressed that the term "emotional plague" carries no defamatory connotation, and it does not refer to any conscious malice. A person is a victim of the plague to the extent that some of her or his own natural aliveness is suppressed. So, to the extent that one does not live through her or his body, that one does not embody aliveness, he or she may manifest the emotional plague. Out of fear of one's own aliveness, the plagued individual is threatened by the manifest aliveness in others. Therefore, he or she tries to discourage or stop others from being alive in the ways that would be threatening to her or him.

Here is how the emotional plague operates in the world of iron. If a man fears his own masculinity and therefore does not express it in the world, he would be suppressing some of his natural aliveness. He would be emotionally plagued. Being confronted with a showy display of bodies which symbolize masculinity would be a painful reminder of his own felt lack. Thus, the competitive weightlifter and the bodybuilder would be unwelcome in his world. They would be reminders of his own inadequacy, fear, and limited aliveness. So, he would try to keep away from lifters, and would want to stop anyone around him from lifting. He would, of course, be the most vehement of critics of the weight sports.

The man who fears masculinity in himself would want to stifle its expression in anyone else, man or woman. Symbols of masculinity such as big muscles and the demonstration of strength would be prime targets for this plagued man. For the woman who fears her masculine side and does not allow herself to experience it, the situation is somewhat different. Likely, she would not be threatened by the expression of masculinity in a man. Since she is a woman, she need not compare herself with a man and be threatened by his masculinity. So, she would not have a need to oppose the weight sports **for men.** Other women who expressed their masculinity through the weights and displayed highly developed muscles could, of course, be a threat. So, this plagued woman would be disapproving of her sisters in the iron world.

I believe that Reich's concept of emotional plague, with its dynamics, is a useful concept for understanding the extreme attitude of opposition towards lifting weights which is sometimes seen. To borrow a phrase from Hamlet, the critic sometimes "protests too much, methinks."

Part II

PSYCHOLOGICAL TECHNIQUES IN LIFTING WEIGHTS

Chapter 8

THE INTERNAL DIALOGUE

IN THIS SECOND part of the book I want to offer some of my insight and understanding as to how psychological knowledge and techniques can be used to enhance the lifting endeavor. These techniques, when understood and appropriately applied, can improve one's lifting performance considerably. Through my personal experimentation and exploration of the techniques which I am offering, I know how effective they can be. At the outset, however, I want to emphasize that **there are no shortcuts, and there is no magic.** There is no substitute for persistent, proper training. Given that one is training appropriately, then these techniques can add to the effects of that training.

The first topic for us to explore is the internal dialogue. Most of the time we are talking to ourselves. While we are awake we are constantly carrying on conversations in our heads. This is the left-brain activity of words. Given the volume of this private dialogue, its effects can be profound. Much of the dialogue is chatter, the utterances of inane verbiage. At the very least this pointless chatter is background noise which uses energy and detracts from incoming sensory signals. So, this chatter cuts down on one's efficiency in living. The situation is analogous to listening to a concert while the people sitting next to you are talking. In the case of the internal chatter, however, the voices are inside one's head.

The quiet mind can be likened to a calm pool of water. With a placid, smooth surface, even the smallest object which falls upon the water will make a ripple. Any impingement on that calm surface will be noted. Very different this is from a pool of disturbed water. Even large objects can smash into the turbulent waters without being noticed for the water's own roilling. And, so it is, with the mind. A calm mind will notice the smallest of sensory signals. But a mind turbulent with senseless chatter will miss all but those signals which are so strong as to stand out even above the mind's own chatter.

The various meditative techniques have as their purpose the quieting of the internal chatter. They are methods which aid one in the practice of being quiet. Since I am the one who speaks inside my head, I can choose to not speak. As **simple** as this is, it is **not easy** for most of us. So, there are many techniques of meditation, some ancient, some modern, which make that simple task somewhat easier to practice. In time, one can develop the skill of quieting.

To be able to come to a state of mental quiet, at will, is a marvelous skill. Its value is immeasurable. For the lifter it has some specific benefits. When tired and in need of sleep, the ability to quiet oneself quickly allows one to go to sleep without delay. It also makes it possible to calm down when overly excited and to get a refreshing break from work and concerns, in a matter of a few minutes. This skill will also have application in the use of imagery, which I will discuss later in this chapter, and in producing the concentration and the "lifting trance" to be presented in a later chapter.

Of the myriad ways of meditating which exist, I have chosen two which I see as especially suited to those in the world of iron. The first is a simple mantra meditation, the second is a form of muscular relaxation.

The mantra meditation which I am suggesting is done as follows. Sit or lie in a comfortable position with your eyes closed. This is to be done, of course, in a quiet, private place. Breathe comfortably and naturally, allowing each inhalation to move into the lower abdomen. Allow a slight pause after each inhalation and after each exhalation. (If this way of breathing is difficult or does not seem natural, just do it as best you can, for now. I will discuss breathing, itself, in great detail in chapter nine.) As you inhale, say inside yourself, "Re-." And, as you exhale, say inside yourself, "-lax." So, with each breath cycle (inhale-pause-exhale-pause) you will say the word "relax," internally. Continue doing this, without hurry, until you feel ready to stop. With practice, you probably will find that this meditation becomes more and more effective in quieting your mental chatter.

Because of our holistic nature, we manifest our being on the mental and the physical planes simultaneously. Mental chatter and muscles held in tension are most often found together. So, as we quiet a tense (chattering) mind, we are quieting a tense body, and vice versa. We can choose to use a technique which focuses primarily on the mental chatter or on one which focuses primarily on the postural tension. Many mantras have traditionally been used, some exotic some more common. For our purposes I chose "Re-lax" for its simplicity and for its pointing to the connection between quieting of mind and relaxing of body.

The second meditation which I want to offer focuses directly on the musculature. In this case, one quiets the mental chatter by systematically directing one's attention to the relaxation of the muscles, one body area at a time. The particular way of doing this is one which I learned many years ago and have used on myself and with psychotherapy clients. It is based on an asana (body posture) of Hatha Yoga known as "savasana," the "corpse pose." I learned this first as savasana and years later in my doctoral study I was exposed to a Western version developed by Edmund Jacobson (1938) and known as "progressive relaxation." What I am about to describe draws both on the savasana of Hatha Yoga and Jacobson's progressive relaxation.

Find a quiet, private place where you can lie down without discomfort. (Once the method is learned well, it can be practiced sitting, as well as lying. But while learning it, and even after it is well known, for greatest benefit, it is practiced in a supine position.) Lie on your back, eyes closed, arms along your sides, and your legs uncrossed. Breathe comfortably. In teaching this method of relaxation I give the following instructions, **speaking slowly** and **pausing for a few moments after each sentence:**

> Imagine a wave of relaxation which is going to spread very slowly over your entire body. Feel the relaxation begin at the tips of your toes and spread up each toe. Allow the relaxation to continue spreading over the soles of your feet and the tops of your feet, up to your ankles. And, now, let the relaxation move up your lower legs to your knees. Over your calves. Over your shins. Feel the relaxation move deeply into your calves. And each time you breathe out, you can relax a little more and a little more. Allow the relaxation to move into your knees. Feel it deep down in the joints. Let the relaxation continue, now, up your legs to your pelvis. The backs of your legs. The outsides of your legs. The insides of your thighs. The fronts of your legs. Each time you breathe out, you can let go a little more. Now, allow the wave of relaxation to move into your pelvis. Let your hips relax. Relax your genitals. Relax your lower abdomen. And, now, the wave of relaxation has spread from the tips of your toes to your waist. And each time you exhale, you can let go a little more and a little more. Allow the relaxation to move up your back now. Your lower back. The middle of your back. Your upper back, up to your neck. And let the relaxation move up your sides to your armpits. Allow the wave of relaxation to spread from your waist up over your upper abdomen and over your chest, up to your

shoulders. Now, let the relaxation spread over your shoulders, and deep down into the joints. Let the wave continue down your arms, over your triceps to your elbows. Over your biceps. And now, down your forearms to your wrists. Allow the relaxation to spread into your hands. The backs of your hands. The palms of your hands. And down each finger to their very tips. Imagine even your fingernails relaxing. The wave of relaxation has now spread from the tips of your toes up to your neck, and down each arm to the tips of your fingers. And, each time you exhale, you can let go a little more, and a little more. Will you now allow the wave of relaxation to spread up your neck? Up the front of your neck, over your throat. Up the sides of your neck. Up the back of your neck and up over the back of your head. Feel the relaxation spread over your scalp. Imagine even your hair relaxing. Let your ears relax. And deep inside your ears. Allow the wave to move on down over your forehead. Let your eyebrows relax. And your eyes. Your nose. And cheeks. Let your lips relax. And your chin. Allow the relaxation to move inside your mouth. Feel your tongue relax. Imagine even your teeth gently relaxing in their sockets. Let your throat relax. And now this very comfortable wave of relaxation has spread over your entire body, from the tips of your toes to the top of your head, and down your arms to the tips of your fingers. And each time you exhale you can relax a little more. Feel the deep, comfortable relaxation.

The pacing of the instructions is very slow, at first. As one practices this method of relaxation one will become more efficient at it. This means both that one can reach the state of full body relaxation more quickly, and that the state reached will be of a more profound relaxation. When beginning this practice it may take ten or fifteen minutes to complete the covering of the whole body. It may help to work with a partner for a few times, having him or her read the above instructions to you. Once you get the feel for the process, you can do it alone, without the words. Rather than hearing the words, you can simply feel your body relax as you move through it systematically with your internal attention. There is a variation discussed both in the yoga and in the progressive relaxation literature which may be helpful if you have difficulty in relaxing your muscles by just thinking of it. The variation is to tense each muscle for a few seconds first, and then let go. One then moves through the body, tensing and relaxing each muscle group one at a time.

If you are in need of sleep when you practice this method of relaxation, you may well fall asleep. When I have had insomnia and used this method to get to sleep, rarely have I remembered getting past my waist!

Once the savasana is well-learned, as well as the mantra meditation discussed earlier, the two can be used together. These two methods used singly or jointly give one a great deal of help in being able to quiet one's mind. Until experienced, it cannot be imagined how very different life seems with a mind that is still.

As energy draining and distracting as mental chatter is, even more devastating are the critical things which one may say to herself or himself. What I am referring to is the negative self talk in which many people engage. It is as if there were an internal critic who is constantly discouraging, depreciating, and, in general, undermining one's self-confidence and sense of well-being. This internal critic may be subtle, just planting seeds of self-doubt by saying things like "You can't do it," "You'll never be able to do that," or "That's probably more than you can do." Or, it may be more blatant and harsh, shouting inside, things like "You stupid idiot, why don't you give up?" or "You're making a fool of yourself." The essence of the internal critic is a voice which criticizes and discourages.

A natural question is "Where does the internal critical voice come from?" The critical voice one hears inside one's head comes from having actually heard such things said when one was young. As a young, dependent child, parents and other parenting figures such as grandparents, other relatives, babysitters, and teachers are sometimes harshly critical. Regardless of their motivation, whether they are ignorant and believe they are helping build the child's character, are insensitive, or are intentionally cruel, the messages of discouragement are given. Sometimes these messages are taken in and believed. To use the psychological term, the critical messages are introjected. It is as if the person then splits inside, forming an internalized critic, which mirrors the external critics, along side the healthy part of the personality. Sometimes the internal critic utters the exact words which the person was told many years before, as a child. In other cases the words are not verbatim, but reflect the essence of what had been said. When the critical message which the child received was nonverbal, then the internal critic provides the words, creating what might have been said if the external critics had used words.

Those readers who suffer from a harsh internal critic know how bothersome it can be. Few people grow up in this society without such an internal critic. For many people, the critic voice is more than just a bother, and actually interferes to a greater or lesser degree with one's performance. For the lifter, this may mean that one discourages one's self from doing one's best, particularly at those times when the stakes are highest, in the contest. Most everyone knows that a cheering crowd can

enhance one's athletic performance. And, a booing crowd, with its negative energy and insults can distract and discourage an athlete. When one
has an active internal critic, it is as if one has brought along a hostile audience, bent on interfering with one's performance.

No matter how well trained and well prepared a lifter is, he or she
will not perform at her or his best as long as her or his internal critic is
operating. In addition, though not as dramatic, the internal critic will
assuredly at times get activated even in training, thus detracting from
the value of that training session.

Remember, the internal critical voice is not natural. It is the continu-
ation of negative introjected messages. And, this is not the voice of con-
structive criticism. It is, rather, a voice that discourages and under-
mines. Its effects are purely deleterious.

In working with psychotherapy patients, I have had a lot of practice
in helping people learn to quiet the voices of their internal critics. So, I
want to offer some guidelines which you, the reader, can use.

The first step in dealing with the internal critic is to **become aware of
it.** Listen carefully to what you say to yourself about yourself. Listen
carefully, and recognize the things which you say which are "put downs,"
discouragements, or in any way statements which make you feel bad or
feel like doing less than your best. Listen for insulting name calling or
any depreciations of your worth or your abilities. Remember, the statements may be harsh and obvious, or they may be subtle and insidious.

Next, **explore** the statement **and experience it.** Listen to the statement word by word, carefully. Say it over and over, if necessary, from the
vantage point of an observer. Let yourself recognize the negative intention of the statement. Notice its inaccuracy, its distortions of truth, and its
nefarious purpose. Feel your reaction to it. Perhaps, imagine how you
would feel if someone else said it to you. In the process of exploring and
experiencing the statement, you may remember who originally gave you
that message, and when. Making this historical connection can be interesting and is usually helpful. It certainly expands one's understanding
of one's self. It is not necessary, however, to make the historical connection
in order to deal with the critical voice. And, making the historical connection does not in and of itself stop the voice. Anamnesis is not therapeusis.
In other words, insight into the origin of the psychological problem is not
the same as the resolving of the problem.

The next step is to **let go of it.** Even though someone else originally
made the critical statement, at this time one is saying it to one's self. As I
pointed out earlier, it is as if the person splits into the internal critic who

says the negative message and the other part of the self who receives the message. Since it is you who is now doing it, you can choose not to do it. You can choose not to say the critical words internally just as surely as you can choose to say something aloud, or not. The critical message has power only insofar as you give it energy. If you say it, you are hanging on to it. But by not saying it, you are letting go of it. This is a solution by "not doing." Or, as some sage once advised, "If you are sticking your finger in your eye and it hurts, stop sticking your finger in your eye!"

As simple as letting go of something is, it is sometimes very difficult. If simply "not doing" is too difficult, then, for now, **do something else.** The something else is to say to yourself something which counters the critical voice. Often, this means saying the opposite. If, for instance, your critical voice is saying, "Dummy!" you can say, "I am not dumb," to counter it. Or, if your internal critic says, "Give up. You'll never be able to do it," you can counter with "I think I can do it; I'll try my best." Such internal counters may sound silly, until you actually try them and experience for yourself how effective they can be.

Eventually, having employed the counter messages enough times, one may find it easier to let go of the critical messages. It is the successful letting go of these messages which gives one freedom from the internal critic.

An example from training may clarify this process of dealing with the interference of an internal critic. Suppose that a lifter finds each time that he or she approaches a training session, he or she feels a draining of enthusiasm. Somehow that special spark disappears as he or she reaches for the bar to start the session. Our lifter is puzzled by this. Having read of the method which I have just discussed, he or she decides to experiment with it. So, next training session our lifter takes the step of awareness. That is, he or she focuses attention on the internal voices as he or she approaches the bar. "Voila!" Our lifter hears an internal voice saying, "Why bother? You'll never be any good at this anyway." Perhaps our lifter recognizes that this voice and this message have a familiar ring. What had been going on outside of awareness is now in awareness.

Given this discovery, this new awareness of the message, our lifter is ready for the second step, exploration and experience. In order to make the second step easier, our lifter may decide to make the voice more vivid. He or she could do this by intentionally repeating the message several times. If our lifter has the benefit of privacy, he or she may choose to say the message aloud, adding to the vividness of the voice. Staying open to the experience, our lifter lets herself or himself feel the

impact of the message. Saying it again and again, our lifter comes to understand very clearly how he or she has been quenching the spark of enthusiasm. The impact of the message becomes obvious and undeniable.
Perhaps our lifter remembers how Dad used to ridicule her or his childhood attempts of athletics, saying, "You'll never be good at that." Our
lifter has now diagnosed the problem. He or she understands the historical origins (Dad's ridicule), but much more importantly, he or she understands the dynamics of the problem (I am telling myself to give up,
that I am not going to be any good at lifting. This discourages me and
takes away my enthusiasm for training.)

Having diagnosed the problem, our lifter is now in a position to do
something to resolve it. So, he or she vows to let the critical message go.
Perhaps our lifter has some degree of success with letting go. The critical
message is gone, most of the time. But, still, during some workouts, the
voice returns with its discouragement. It seems to come back on days
when our lifter is a bit tired, a bit rushed, or in some other way not at
her or his best.

The persistence of the critical voice calls for doing something else, instead of energizing the voice. So, our lifter creates a counter voice. Each
time that he or she hears the internal critic, our lifter says back, "I like
this, and I am getting better and better at it!" He or she says this with
force and conviction. And, he or she repeats it until the critical voice is
quieted. Our lifter does this countering consistently. Every time the
critical voice is heard, it is thoroughly countered.

After several weeks of successful countering, the critical voice is but a
rare whisper. At this point our lifter finds that he or she can simply let
go. The introjected voice of discouragement has been expelled. Now our
lifter trains with enthusiasm, undampened by an internal critic.

If one uses this method diligently for several weeks and is not successful in quieting the voice of the internal critic, then I would suggest getting some professional help. A psychotherapist can be of immense help
in these more resistant situations.

Thus far in the present chapter I have discussed the quieting of internal chatter and the quieting of the voice of the internal critic. If one is
bothered by internal chatter and an internal critic, as many, perhaps
even most people are, then the use of the methods outlined can make a
dramatic change in one's life. One's training and performance in competition can be enhanced remarkably. With the banishing of the mental
chatter comes a clarity of mind, which allows for both keener perception
and keener thought. And, the energy which had gone into maintaining

Figure 10

Quieting the Internal Critic

Step I: Awareness

(Listen carefully to your internal voices
and become aware of what your internal
critic is saying.)

Step II: Exploration and Experience

(Repeat the critical message clearly and completely
and experience your emotional reaction to it.)

Step III: Letting Go   **Step IV: Doing Something Else**

(Choose not to say the   (Say something which counters
critical message.)   the critical message every
                                time it appears.)

The internal critic is quiet.

the chatter is freed for other uses. With the quieting of the internal critic comes a release from negative forces, a freedom from the heavy mantle of discouragement and disrespect.

Once the mental chatter is quieted and the voice of the internal critic is quieted, you are ready to learn to use self-talk as a positive force. If in quieting the internal critic you used counter messages, then you have had some experience with positive self-talk. I do recommend that you have grown to the level that you can control mental chatter and your internal critic before you begin to use the following method. Otherwise, much of your efforts will be lost. Mental chatter can distract and drown out positive self-talk, and a strong internal critic can negate it, leaving it as empty words.

The particular method which I am about to present involves the creation and use of a mantra. The mantra will encapsulate the essence of the positive message which one would benefit from hearing. There are several guidelines for the creation and use of the mantra. I suggest that the reader follow these guidelines carefully until you gain familiarity with the method. Then, if you wish, you can experiment with variations.

First, the idea is to tell yourself something which would serve to motivate you to do the very best of which you are capable. It will not work, in the long run, to tell yourself anything that is not true. Stay within realistic limits. Thus, you would not tell yourself that you could lift a weight which is fifty pounds in excess of your best. Nor would you tell yourself that you are the most awesome physique of all time. You might, with beneficial effect, however, tell yourself that you could lift five more pounds than your previous best, or that you can do your best poses.

Second, the mantra is most effective when it is short, simple, and pithy. "This is my chance to do my best deadlift ever, and I am confident that the probability of my success is exceedingly high." This preceding is **not** a mantra. The following is—"I can do it!" Excess verbiage, even if it contains qualifiers which make a technically more complete and accurate statement serve only to detract from the essential message. Again, keep the mantra brief, simply worded, and to the point.

Third, use the mantra over and over. The repetitiousness of the mantra is a key to its success. Remember, this is a mantra to be chanted, not a statement to convey new information. Its purpose is to motivate, not to inform. So, repeat the mantra over and over until you feel its effect. When you have chanted it long enough, you will know it. Something inside you will shift, and you will recognize it. This criterion of an internal shift is far more effective than is the counting of the repetitions or the timing of the chanting by the clock. It is an internal, subjective experience which is sought, so external, objective criteria such as repetitions or clock time miss the point. So, find your rhythm and keep chanting until you feel the internal shift. That could take six repetitions or sixty.

Fourth, use the mantra until it is no longer needed, and if it suggests or evolves into a new one, then use the new one. This often happens. One may wear out a mantra on a given occasion, to find that a new mantra then appears spontaneously.

Having given this overview of the mantra method, I want to deal with some more details of the wording. Just as one will recognize subjectively when a mantra has been chanted enough, one will recognize subjectively when the wording is correct. We could create several mantras all of the same gist, but only one would sound right to the user. This is a very subjective experience by which one recognizes the best wording for herself or himself. This means that one has to experiment. Try several alternative wordings until it feels just right.

Another interesting feature of the wording of the mantra is that it may be more effective when stated in the positive form or it may be more effective when stated in negative form. In dealing with a negative thought or feeling, often times stating the mantra in the negative form is more potent. For example, a powerlifter may be having trouble concentrating on his bench press because of anticipating his opening deadlift. So, he or she could either use a mantra whose essence is "I can stay in the here-and-now," or one whose essence is "I don't have to jump ahead." Many people find this latter form works better as a starting point. This is a case of negating something negative. Very often, I have found, the negatively stated mantra will evolve into a positively stated one, in a while. So, after chanting "I don't have to jump ahead," for awhile, one may evolve to "I can stay in the here-and-now."

The method of the mantra can also be used effectively in centering oneself in a higher state of consciousness. So, if one has chosen lifting as a path for personal growth, one can employ a mantra to help motivate herself or himself to stay on the path. If, for instance, one were to find one's self strongly attached to the outcome of a meet, distorting one's perspective by valuing winning too highly, he or she might use a mantra. "I don't have to win in order to be happy," or "I don't have to be attached to outcome," are candidates for the negatively stated mantra. In positive form one might try, "I can enjoy the process," or, simply, "Have fun!"

Allow me a more detailed example of the use of the mantra method by a lifter. Imagine a male bodybuilder who approaches a physique contest with great fear. Feeling afraid, he might chant to himself, backstage, "I don't have to be afraid." He might chant while pumping up or while oiling his skin. After several minutes he begins to feel excited, rather than afraid. He then chants to himself, "I can be excited." Just before going on stage he chants, "I can do my best." Having placed high enough in the ranks to be invited into a "pose down," he starts to feel very attached to winning, hearing himself saying, "I've **got** to win this, or else." Recognizing this, he begins to chant, "I'll do my best, but I don't have to win." Just before stepping onto the stage for the "pose down" he chants, "Have fun, look good!"

The difficult part of presenting an example of the use of mantras is that there are so many variations on their use. The possibilities for the effective use of the mantra are incredible, limited only by the user's lack of creativity. The basic principles are: stay within reality; keep the mantra short, simple, pithy; find just the right words; and use it until you wear it out.

As powerfully effective as the mantra method is, there is another method which is also very potent in enhancing lifting and posing performance. This is the method of mental imagery. The mantra is, of course verbal. Imagery is the non-verbal counterpart.

If words are the language of the left-brain, imagery is the language of the right brain. Some psychologists, in discussing dreams, have spoken of dream imagery as the preferred language of the unconscious. So, by using mental imagery, the lifter is engaging the right brain and using the language of the unconscious.

I want to distinguish two types of mental imagery. First, is visual imagery, in which one "sees" scenes in the mind's eye. This is like watching a movie, except the movie is going on inside one's head. Second, is kinesthetic imagery. In this case it is body sensations which are imagined. In both types of imagery, one's focus is on one's internal world. The outside world is let go of, as one turns inward to a private world of images.

Let us explore the use of visual imagery, first. Visual imagery can be used both for the enhancement of one's training and the enhancement of one's performance in competition. Here is how to do it. Get in a comfortable position, close your eyes, stop any mental chatter, and see yourself in your mind's eye. Watch yourself perform. Watch carefully. Concentrate. **See yourself as vividly as possible** executing the particular movement, be that an exercise lift, a competitive lift, or a pose. Rehearse the movement over and over. See yourself from different angles — front view, back view, left side view, right side view, looking up at yourself as if you were performing on a transparent platform, looking down at yourself from above, and various angles in between these. Be like a television camera operator, moving closer, moving farther away, zooming in, and fading back. Change the distance and change the angle. Explore thoroughly with your mind's eye. You can also slow down the action. The slow motion visualization may allow you to see something that you missed when you were visualizing at natural speed. **As you do this visual imagery, you are rehearsing your performance.** You are practicing. This method is especially helpful in your preparation for competition. You can watch yourself successfully making your lifts or smoothly flowing through your posing routine.

Key to the effectiveness of the use of visual imagery is the visualization of a successful performance. **See yourself in impeccable form.** See yourself succeed with the lift in perfect form. See yourself pose smoothly, gracefully and in perfect form.

In the case of the other type of mental imagery, the image is not visual, but is kinesthetic. Rather than "seeing" yourself perform, you "feel" yourself perform. In order to do this, again, make yourself comfortable, close your eyes, and stop any mental chatter. Now, in your mind/body, feel yourself performing the movements. Imagine yourself doing the exercise, doing the competitive lift, or doing the pose. **Feel the body sensations as vividly as possible** as you execute the movements. Get the "feel" in your mind/body. **Rehearse your performance over and over.** "Feel" every detail. In the case of lifting, "feel" the steel in your hands, "feel" the motion of every body part, and "feel" the resistance of the weight. Be realistic. Don't make the resistance either too little or too much. Do **"feel" yourself in impeccable form, succeeding.** If you are mentally rehearsing a posing routine, "feel" the movement of every body part. "Feel" the rhythm and timing of your moves, your balance, and the strain of flexing.

When you perform in your mind, using visual imagery or kinesthetic imagery, you are rehearsing for your performance in the outside world. **Whatever you do in your private mental world will be mirrored in your outside, physical world.** This does not imply a one to one correspondence between the two worlds, of course. I could rehearse a 500 pound squat in my mind for a half-hour a day for the next three months, but I would be very unlikely to be able to do it, and would probably injure myself trying (my best squat was 325 lb. at a body weight of about 157 lb., in my early forties). **Imagery rehearsal will not allow you to do more than you are physically able to do.** Although a truism, this is worth pondering. Most of the time, however, we do far less than we are physically capable of doing. Imagery is a method for assisting one to approach her or his potential performance. The images you use will tend to produce the physical conditions and overt performance that correspond to them.

There is an important implication to what I have just pointed out in the above paragraph. That is, imagine only the correct and desired action. Never rehearse what you do not want to do. If you rehearse what you do not want to do, enough, that will surely be yours.

More specifically, it is **how** you do your successful performance that is to be rehearsed. This means careful attention to every detail of the desired performance. The same neurological pathways are excited by the imagery as by the actual performance. Earlier, when I was discussing Edmund Jacobson's work with "progressive relaxation," I spoke of the effect of relaxation thoughts on the muscles themselves. The reverse is also true. In his research, Jacobson demonstrated that when one images an

activity there are "micro-movements" in the muscles that are involved in
that activity. These muscular micro-movements show that one is practicing the performance by exciting the neurological pathways that will be
involved in the overt performance, even when one appears relaxed and
motionless to an observer.

By repeatedly practicing the desired performance through imagery,
one is "overlearning" the action, to use a psychological term. Overlearning means practice beyond the point at which one has learned to do
something correctly one time. A performance which is overlearned is
less likely to be forgotten. It becomes so familiar that even under pressure it is well remembered and will tend to come to one automatically.
How much one needs to practice imagery for optimal effect depends on
many individual and situational factors. So, it is best to experiment with
it oneself and find through one's own experience what works best. Just to
give you some orientation for starting your own experimentation, there
is some consensus among sports psychologists that five to ten minutes of
imagery, twice a day is optimal for most athletes. What is best for you
may vary from this guideline.

In actual practice, sometimes visual imagery and kinesthetic imagery
can be combined. One may wish to visualize herself or himself in impeccable performance while at the same time creating strong kinesthetic
feeling of that performance. My suggestion, however, is that you perfect
the techniques of visual imagery and kinesthetic imagery first.
Otherwise, the two techniques may interfere with each other, splitting
your attention and thereby reducing the vividness of your images. Less
vivid images would, of course, diminish the impact of the methods.

An interesting adjunct to the basic methods of visual and kinesthetic
imagery which I have presented, is the use of a metaphorical image. A
powerlifter working on perfecting her or his form in the deadlift might
"see" or "feel" herself or himself as a huge, powerful bull pulling a heavy
boulder. An Olympic lifter might liken her or his jerk to a space shuttle
rocket taking off, "seeing" herself or himself as that rocket or "feeling"
like that rocket. A physique contestant wanting a smoother more fluid
transition from one pose to another might pick a slowly flowing river as
her or his metaphor, "seeing" and "feeling" it. The useful metaphors are
endless. Again, only one's lack of creativity limits this. The idea is to
pick a metaphor for what one wants to learn or polish or accomplish.
Then, through one's visual and kinesthetic imagery, explore the metaphor, experience it, be it. By doing so, one can activate unconscious
knowledge, bring into awareness potential experiences which enhance

one's intentional performance. Let yourself go with this technique. Use your intuition in finding metaphors, and live them out in visual and kinesthetic imagery. In doing so you will inevitably tap into archetypal images, bringing that power to your activity.

It is now well accepted by sports psychologists that mental imagery is a powerful tool for improving athletic performance. Much careful research backs up this acceptance. And, a large number of successful athletes report the importance of mental imagery in their training programs. Note that for the lifter, mental imagery is not a substitute for actual lifting. It is a way of helping overlearn the coordination and timing of actual movements, of activating muscles at will, and of infusing one's actual performance with a spark of inspiration. In addition, mental imagery can be put to good use when one is unable to lift because of injury or environmental circumstances.

Mental imagery certainly has an important place in one's training. I want to put it in perspective in terms of the psychological levels at which one can train. I will do this by means of a model of Psychological Levels of Training which I have developed.

The first level of training involves only thinking and talking. So, this is an abstract level of training. It is a left-brain activity, one in which verbal symbols are used. The **Thinking** level involves such activities as planning one's training program and one's workout, thinking about what exercises, what sequences, what weights, what number of sets, and

Figure 11

Psychological Levels of Training

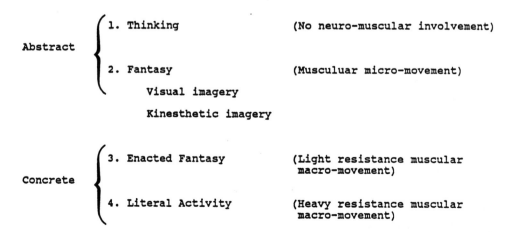

Abstract	{	1. Thinking	(No neuro-muscular involvement)
		2. Fantasy	(Musculuar micro-movement)
		Visual imagery	
		Kinesthetic imagery	
Concrete	{	3. Enacted Fantasy	(Light resistance muscular macro-movement)
		4. Literal Activity	(Heavy resistance muscular macro-movement)

what number of repetitions to use, and with what frequency to do this. So this level is concerned with **what to do;** it is the level of planning. In addition, this level involves the use of the techniques presented earlier in this chapter for quieting mental chatter, quieting the internal critic and using self-talk as a positive force. So, all of the methods of quieting negative talk, be it distracting chatter or demoralizing criticism, and of bringing forth encouragement and support through positive self-talk belong to this first level of training. It involves the abstract — the use of words or the quieting of words. At this level of training there is no activation of the skeletal muscles, except, of course, the muscles involved in speech. There is no activating neuro-muscular involvement of the "lifting muscles."

The second level of training is the **Fantasy** level. This level involves the use of imagery, visual imagery and kinesthetic imagery. Therefore, this level, just as the Thinking level before it, is an abstract level. But, unlike the Thinking level, it involves neuro-muscular activation, albeit in the form of muscular micro-movements. The use of fantasy is, as we have seen, for the purpose of rehearsal.

With the third level, **Enacted Fantasy,** we move into the realm of concrete activity. Not only is there neuro-muscular activation, but the actual physical actions are taken. The muscular movements are now macro-movements, but with very light resistance. A light weight is used, the actual movements are enacted, but with the fantasy of the actual event. For example, when I was competing in Olympic style lifting I would sometimes enact fantasies of contests. I would imagine I was stepping onto the lifting platform as I took an actual step or two. I would see the crowd, the judges and the loaded bar in my mind's eye. Then I would address an actual empty bar, or on occasion even a broomstick, in the way I actually addressed the Olympic bar in competition. (In a succeeding chapter I will discuss the "addressing of the bar.") I would then perform a press, or snatch, or clean and jerk with the empty bar or broomstick. As I did so I would "feel" the strain of the lift, "see" the head judge make his thumbs up gesture, "hear" the announcer excitedly shout, "The lift is good!" and "hear" the crowd cheer. Sometimes, when a workout is dragging, I enact a mini-fantasy, imagining that whatever exercise I am about to do is a record attempt in an important contest. Try that the next time you need a boost to get through your last set of curls!

The fourth level of training is **Literal Activity.** Here, again, we are in the realm of concrete activity with muscular macro-movements, but with heavy resistance. This is the actual, literal, practice of lifting.

In explaining these four levels, I have used lifting as the content. Clearly, though, one can look at posing through these levels. There is the planning of a posing routine (Thinking), deciding what poses in what sequence for what period of time to what music, if any. Then, there is the Fantasy work of "seeing" the routine and "feeling" the routine through visual and kinesthetic imagery, respectively. Next comes the enactment of this fantasy, the pretending to be on the posing dais and "hearing" the applause as one enacts parts of the routine and at various tempos. Finally, comes the Literal Activity, the actual posing, done just as in a contest with one's coach or friends offering their critiques.

If the first level of training, Thinking, focuses on **what to do,** as discussed above, the second, third, and fourth levels, Fantasy, Enacted Fantasy, and Literal Activity, focus on **how to do it.** In moving through the four levels we progress from the abstract to the concrete, from no neuro-muscular involvement through muscular micro-movements to muscular macro-movements of light and heavy resistance. There is a logic in this progression. **I submit that optimal results are obtained only when the lifter gives adequate attention to all four levels.** By doing so, the lifter honors her or his holistic nature, involving mind (both as left-brain manifestation and as right-brain manifestation) and body planes of being.

Chapter 9

CENTERING, CHARGING, GROUNDING, DISCHARGING

BEING "CENTERED" is as important as it is difficult to put into words. It is an experience, which once known, is easily recognized by its occurrence or non-occurrence. When centered, one feels alive, free from distracting tension, and able to focus on whatever is of interest. Thus, the act of centering involves enlivenment through adequate **breathing, relaxing,** and **concentrating,** without effort.

Before moving into the pragmatics of breathing techniques, I believe some further philosophical framing of the experience of being centered is in order. This philosophical understanding will put the techniques in a context which will give them greater meaning.

Our experience in the world involves three dimensions, namely, space, time and awareness. That is, we experience ourselves in a physical place, at a particular time, and with a particular level of awareness. We locate ourselves as "here," as opposed to "there." The space dimension involves the point where I am as contrasted with to my left, to my right, in front of me, behind me, above me, or below me. I am "here," as opposed to all the other places "there." We also locate ourselves "now," as opposed to "then." This dimension of time involves the ever-moving moment of the "now" which moves from the "then" known as "before" toward the "then" which is known as "after." Thus, "past" and "future" form the poles of the time dimension. Awareness forms a dimension from vague or cloudy to precise and clear. And, awareness involves my sensory systems. Thus, awareness is based on my embodiment, my existing as an organismic being. In summary, we might then say that the parameters of existence are extension (space), duration (time), and embodiment (awareness). Admittedly, this is quite abstract. But, bear with me a little longer and you will see some very practical applications of this heady material to the bodily act of pumping iron.

Although I exist at a particular place, at a particular time, and with a particular level of awareness, it is possible for me to diminish the vividness or "realness" of that existential moment. We as humans are able to cloud our awareness through a myriad of psychological mechanisms, as well as through chemical means. (To describe the psychological mechanisms of clouding awareness is beyond the scope of this present chapter. If you are interested in reading about those mechanisms, I refer you to one of my earlier books, *The Body in Psychotherapy* [Smith, 1985]). We are also able, through fantasy, to leave the present time and present place. Fantasy is of immense value to the lifter, as I have shown in the previous chapter. However, one can get lost in fantasy, moving without consciously intending to, into a world of fantasy. Such unintentional "daydreaming" can decrease one's effectiveness in the "here-and-now."

I am centered when I am in my body in the here-and-now. When I am centered, I am at my most powerful and my most effective, in the actual world. Think of these things. If I have psychologically left my body and gone off in fantasy, my awareness is not with what is actual, and whatever movements I make are not guided by full awareness and attention. I can be effective in the world only to the extent that I am here and now and embodied. The less I am here, the less I am now, the less I am embodied, the less powerful and effective I am. I cannot do tomorrow's workout today! I can rehearse a workout. And, as I have discussed, this rehearsal can be of great value. But, the rehearsal is not tomorrow's actual workout; it is my having an intentional fantasy in the here and now. My dealing with the actual, physical reality can only take place in the actual, present time and place. In some ways this seems so obvious. But, even if it is a truism, it is easily forgotten or ignored in actual training and competition.

Let me emphasize, **one trains better and competes better when centered.** For this reason, I want to explore some methods of becoming centered.

One of the most powerful methods for centering is through focusing on one's breathing. We have already explored how breathing deeply and slowly into one's abdomen, with slight pauses after each inhalation and each exhalation can be calming and relaxing. Such calming and relaxing can be centering when one is tense, nervous, "up tight." Tension in the muscles and chatter in the mind move one off center, not to mention introjected negative messages. To center, therefore, may involve the stopping of introjected negative messages, stopping mental chatter, relaxing the muscles, and the use of an affirmative mantra. Methods for doing these things have been presented previously. In addition, and central to the act of centering, is the slow breathing, low in the abdomen.

Not only can focused breathing be a path to a relaxed centeredness, but it can also lead to a state of high energy. This latter state is of immense value for the lifter, in training, and even more so in competition. To understand how this works, I will delve into the bioenergetics of breathing.

As a starting point, think of yourself as an energy system. As an embodied being, you take in nutrients, metabolize them, and thus provide energy for work and materials for growth and repair. Your energy is provided by your nutrition as it is transformed by your metabolic fires. Your breathing provides the oxygen which regulates the metabolic fires. Like the damper on a wood burning stove, your breathing regulates how much oxygen is available and, therefore, how hot and how fast the fuel is burned.

So, as breathing is altered to provide a greater supply of oxygen, one creates a higher charge of energy. One can breathe in a manner which is analogous to a closed damper, an open damper, or an open damper with a bellows pumping in air, depending on the organism's requirements. It is this latter way of breathing which charges the organism with energy.

Let us consider the biomechanics of breathing. Normal, relaxed breathing is an involuntary rhythmic activity controlled by the autonomic nervous system. On the average, when one is awake and relaxed, one takes fourteen to eighteen breaths per minute. This amounts to twenty or twenty-five thousand breaths each day. One of the fascinating things about breathing is that one can override the autonomic control and make breathing a conscious, voluntary activity. By doing so, one can determine, within a certain range, both the rate of breathing and its depth. In normal breathing there is a smooth, rhythmic action which involves the entire length of the body. Inhalation consists of an outward movement of the belly as the abdominal muscles relax and the diaphragm contracts. The chest expands. The pelvis rocks slightly so that the sacrum moves back. At the same time the neck arches back, slightly. So, on inspiration there is a slight arching back of the entire torso, reducing the distance between the cranial and sacral ends. When deep and full, this wave of inspiration can be felt from the head to the pelvis, and even down to the feet. After a brief pause, this wave is reversed. Thus, on exhalation, as the diaphragm relaxes, the abdomen moves back in place from its protruded position and the chest relaxes from its expansion. The pelvis rocks forward and the head returns to its resting position, with the arch taken out of the neck. On expiration the cranial-sacral distance is increased. There is a brief pause, again, as one breathing cycle is completed.

What I have just described is **abdominal or diaphragmatic breathing.** Let us consider this type of breathing once more, from a somewhat more technical point of view. The diaphragm is a dome shaped muscle attaching to the ribs and separating the thoracic cavity from the abdominal cavity. In its contracted position, the diaphragm flattens out, lowering the peak of the dome toward the abdomen. Therefore, when the diaphragm contracts, there is an increase in the vertical diameter of the thoracic cavity, and thereby a reduction in the intrathoracic pressure. Since the air pressure outside the body is then greater than the air pressure inside the thoracic cavity, the result is an inflow of air through the nose or mouth. On exhalation the diaphragm relaxes to its more dome shaped position while the recoil of the stretched costal cartilages and stretched lungs and the weight of the thoracic wall increase the intrathoracic pressure. With the air pressure greater in the thoracic cavity than the air pressure outside, air is forced out the nose or mouth. In normal, quiet respiration, then, inhalation is active (the diaphragm contracts) and exhalation is passive (the diaphragm relaxes).

Once again, it is this abdominal or diaphragmatic breathing which characterizes a calm, relaxed state. In that state, abdominal breathing will take place automatically, without one's attention and without conscious control. Therefore, when one wants to bring about a calm, relaxed state, it is this type of breathing which one can do, intentionally. **To center, do slow, deep, abdominal breathing.**

The other pattern of breathing is one of forced respiration, known as **thoracic or costal breathing.** In thoracic breathing the external intercostal muscles and several synergic muscles actually force an expansion of the rib cage. They literally pull the chest into an expanded position. With this expansion of the rib cage, there is, of course, a reduction of the intrathoracic pressure. Now, with a greater relative air pressure outside, air rushes into the lungs through the nose or mouth. Once again, as was true for abdominal breathing, the phase of inhalation is active, involving the contraction of muscles. In thoracic breathing, however, the phase of exhalation is also active. The abdominal muscles, internal intercostal muscles, serratus posterior inferior, and quadratus lumborum all contract, thus reducing the size of the thoracic cavity, and squeezing the air out. In thoracic breathing the chest pumps like a bellows, sucking air in and forcing it out.

Thoracic breathing is natural and automatic during strenuous muscular exertion. When one is exerting physically, abdominal breathing with its passive phase of exhalation is too slow to provide for an adequate supply of oxygen. What is needed is forced breathing, the pumping of air provided by the active inhalations and exhalations of thoracic breathing. This allows for a more rapid exchange of oxygenated and deoxygenated air, bringing in oxygen and expelling carbon dioxide.

So, as one moves from a state of relaxation and quiet to a state of muscular exertion, one's breathing will naturally and automatically shift from abdominal breathing to thoracic breathing. As the organism requires a faster supply of oxygen, it will make this shift in the pattern of breathing without requiring any conscious intention to do so.

One can intentionally shift to thoracic breathing when one is not making any muscular exertion. Try that in a moment. Stand up. Take five rapid thoracic breaths. Make each inhalation as full as possible, and each exhalation as full as possible. **Suck** the air in and **blow** the air out. Be sure to pause, momentarily at the end of each inhalation and at the end of each exhalation. Do this, now. ...What body sensations do you feel? What I just experienced as I did this intentional forced breathing was as follows: an "aliveness" in my hands which quickly spread up my arms, over my shoulder and chest, and over the rest of my body; a sensation of heat; an increased vividness of vision; a feeling of alertness. In a word, I was charged. I repeated this demonstration, taking ten breaths. This time, in addition to what I had experienced before, I became light headed. The conventional medical term for that latter experience is "hyperventilation." The bioenergetic description is "overcharged." To use a metaphor, in the first experience I was like a "revved-up" motor, whereas in the second experience I was "over-revved."

So, when the lifter wants to raise her or his energy level in preparation for lifting, she or he can take several big, fast breaths, breathing costally. **To charge, do fast, full thoracic breathing.**

An interesting breathing situation exists when one is anxious. The anxious breathing pattern is a fast thoracic pattern, but in the absence of muscular exertion. Also, the inhalation is emphasized. The exhalation and the pause following the exhalation are de-emphasized, giving anxious breathing its characteristic shallow, rather gasping quality. To get a feel for the anxious breathing pattern, so as to recognize it and distinguish it from the natural costal breathing during exertion and the intentional costal breathing used to build a high energy charge, try the following. Take quick, small, gasping breaths high in your chest. Exhale only slightly, without pause before inhaling again. Emphasize the inhalation. Do this for half a minute or so and see how you feel. Having just done this myself, I feel "short of breath," my heart is pounding, and I feel uneasy. In a word, I feel anxious.

So as not to remain anxious, and to show how efficient and effective intentional slow, full abdominal breathing can be in getting centered, use this pattern of diaphragmatic breathing for a couple of minutes.

Relatively speaking, regardless of the pattern of breathing, be it costal or diaphragmatic, the inhalation is the charging phase of the breath cycle, while the exhalation is the discharging phase. That is, as I inhale, I take in the oxygen-laden air to support my metabolism. And, as I do so, my muscles tense for action, again, relative to the phase of exhalation. As I exhale, I let out and let go. In the context of thoracic breathing during exertion, the letting go is forceful. I blow the air out of my lungs, and exert a muscular effort. The exhalation phase of thoracic breathing gives support for maximal muscular exertion. If I am doing thoracic breathing to build an energy charge, I make no muscular exertion as I forcefully exhale. By charging with each inhalation, but not discharging through muscular exertion, I build and build the energy charge either until I am ready to discharge through muscular exertion or else I become overcharged. In the context of abdominal breathing, my letting go means the relaxing of muscular tonus, rather than muscular exertion. Recall, that in the previous chapter when I gave directions for savasana, I repeated several times, "Each time you exhale you can relax a little more." Each increment of relaxation is realized on the exhalation. And, with each exhalation the discharge equals or exceeds the charge. Thus, greater and greater relaxation is experienced.

So, inhalation is charging (low charge in the case of diaphragmatic breathing, high charge in the case of costal breathing). And, exhalation is discharging (muscular relaxation in the case of diaphragmatic breathing, muscular action in the case of costal breathing during exertion). When charging with intentional, forced costal breathing, the discharge accompanying the exhalation is far less than the charge accompanying each inhalation, and thus the build up of a high energy charge.

As a Zen Master is said to have stated this, breathing in binds and combines, holding the breath makes everything go right, and breathing out loosens and completes by overcoming all limitations (Herrigel, 1953). He was speaking about the role of breathing in the Zen practice of archery.

It behooves the lifter to understand well the bioenergetics of breathing. By knowing this, he or she is better able to center himself or herself, and build a high energy charge intentionally, in preparation for a hard set, a limit lift, or a demanding posing routine. For review, I am summarizing the bioenergetics of breathing in Figure 12.

An understanding of the above material makes it clear that the organism's healthy bioenergetic process is a dynamic one, constantly flowing between periods of **quiet relaxation** and **muscular exertion,** as intentionally influenced by periods of **charging** and of **centering.** When relaxed, one can charge, in preparation for muscular exertion. When

Figure 12

Bioenergetics of Breathing

Type of Breathing	Energetics	Organismic State
Automatic Abdominal (Diaphragmatic)	Inspirational charge = Expirational discharge	Quiet relaxation
Intentional, slow, deep Abdominal (Diaphragmatic)	Inspirational charge < Expirational discharge	Centering
Automatic Thoracic (Costal)	Inspirational charge = Expirational and Muscular discharge	Muscular Exertion
Intentional, fast, full Thoracic (Costal)	Inspirational charge > Expirational discharge	Charging
Uncontrolled, fast, shallow Thoracic (Costal)	Inspirational charge > Expirational and Muscular discharge	Anxious

left with an excess charge after muscular exertion (overcharged), one can move toward relaxation by means of centering, and so forth.

Anxiety presents a special challenge. When mild, it may be handled by an intentional shift to slow, deep, abdominal breathing. When this seems too difficult, an alternative is to shift intentionally to a fuller thoracic breathing (charging) and begin some muscular exertion. Through the expirational and muscular discharge of physical activity one can process much of the energy charge, leaving one in an easier position for then centering. In a contest, for instance, if one feels anxious, and centering breathing and a mantra do not seem to be working, perhaps some fast pacing would help, followed by centering breathing. And, of course, after the first lift or first round of posing, one has usually processed sufficient energy that only a little centering breathing is needed, if that. If anxiety is a too frequent or too severe problem, the lifter is well advised to seek the consultation of a psychotherapist.

Returning to the bioenergetics of lifting, there is an optimal level of charge for the task at hand. A warm-up set of an exercise requires less of a charge than does a later, heavy set. A maximum lift begs for even a greater charge. So, an undercharge presents a problem. The solution to this problem is to build a higher charge through appropriate breathing. It is also possible to lift while overcharged. And this, too, presents a problem for the lifter. The solution is to lower the energy level by doing some centering—appropriate breathing, muscle relaxation, and, if necessary, the other methods covered.

This phenomenon of an optimal level of arousal is worthy of further exploration. In psychology, it is known as the Yerkes-Dodson Law. In a now classical experiment performed by Yerkes and Dodson in 1908, it was demonstrated that people performed best with an intermediate level of arousal, with performance suffering with either a lower or higher level. Many subsequent studies have been done, investigating a wide range of arousal levels and a wide variety of performance tasks. In general, the evidence shows that for a given person in a given situation there is a level of arousal which supports a maximum performance; with a level of arousal which falls short of that optimal zone, or exceeds it, performance is less than maximal. Furthermore, the more complex the performance task, the lower the optimal level of arousal. So, in scientific terms, the relationship between arousal and performance is curvilinear with optimal performance at an intermediate level. The more complex the task, the more the peak of the performance curve shifts towards the lower end of the arousal axis.

The Yerkes-Dodson Law has some very important implications for lifters. In applying it to the world of iron the following implications emerge.

First, there are individual differences in optimal level of arousal based on the difficulty level of that task, for that individual. For example, a given powerlifter may find the squat to involve more difficult coordinations than the bench press. For that lifter, then, the optimal level of arousal for the squat will be lower than for the bench press. If he or she were to charge to the level that is optimal for bench pressing, in preparation for squatting, his or her squat would suffer due to a disorganized or inefficient performance. An overcharge, remember, is uncentering. The overcharged lifter's coordination and timing are off, and her or his awareness is clouded. On the other hand, if this lifter bench pressed with the level of charge which would be optimal for the squat, he or she would be undercharged and not put out a maximal exertion.

Second, the more one practices the performance, the easier it gets. This is a truism, but it has a special meaning in the context of the Yerkes-Dodson Law. As the lifter practices to the point of overlearning her or his performance, then it becomes automatic, or nearly so. Timing and coordination do not, then, require as much attention. Awareness can be focused on other things. Therefore, the optimal level of arousal is raised, and one can perform with a greater charge of energy. The result is a stronger performance. Simply stated, a higher charge will increase performance on an overlearned task.

Third, there are differences in the optimal level of arousal for different lifting tasks based on their skill complexity. As a generalization, for instance, it seems clear that with respect to timing and coordination, a well choreographed posing routine is more complex than is Olympic style lifting, and, in turn Olympic style lifting is more complex than powerlifting. So, the optimal level of arousal is lowest for posing, higher for Olympic style lifting, and highest for powerlifting.

Fourth, it is vitally important that the lifter know herself or himself well enough to be able to judge when the charge experienced is optimal for the performance about to be undertaken. This may be one of the crucial differences between a really good competitor and a so-so lifter.

Keep in mind that charging is a faster process than centering. It takes only a few seconds of forced thoracic breathing by a well centered lifter in order to build a high charge of energy. If overcharged, however, it may take several minutes of muscular relaxation, use of mantra, and slow diaphragmatic breathing to once again feel centered. But, again, knowing one's self will allow a fine tuning of arousal level through the creative use of charging and centering techniques.

As a side note, I want to comment on some of the styles of "psyching-up" for a lift. Two of the most dramatic which I have seen, and which have become fairly popular in powerlifting circles, are screaming and having one's face slapped. Screaming requires forced thoracic breathing. And, it emphasizes the exhalation phase. So screaming can be a good way to charge. I believe that it is the exhalation-emphasized, forced thoracic breathing which is the most important aspect in this method of getting charged. The sound may, of course, add to the adrenaline rush. Face slapping can also get the adrenaline flowing. I personally find that "getting mad" doesn't help my lifting. For me, getting mad is un-centering, and distracts from my lifting concentration, coordination and timing.

Several writers of the iron world have observed that most highly accomplished lifters build their charge in a manner that shows almost an outward calm. They tend not to scream, yell, growl, or have their faces slapped. The charge is building inside to the point of a precisely timed optimal explosion.

Ultimately, the style of "psyching-up" is a pragmatic and esthetic choice. Find what is effective for you, and what seems right. Importantly, though, practice your style of charging and centering. Practice these techniques until you can count on them when you really need them. The posing dais and the lifting platform are not the places to try out new techniques for the first time.

That being undercharged will lower one's performance is obvious and smacks of common sense. But, to really know and understand the dynamic of a lowered performance because of being overcharged requires some experience and careful observation. Especially in a competitive situation, one can observe the results of being overcharged. Once in a contest I remember "psyching" myself up as far as I could before my final clean and jerk. I rushed to the bar, cleaned it quickly, recovered, and tossed it over my head...and backward. As it crashed to the floor, I hardly knew what had happened. I was so overcharged that my awareness was impaired and I totally missed the "groove" of the jerk. My explosion of energy was certainly adequate, but it was not controlled, not focused, or, as I said, not in the "groove."

Some time back I was watching a women's powerlifting meet, doing research for the present book. I saw two good examples of the effects of overarousal. First, a lifter went through her "psyching-up" ritual, only to go charging to the bench and lift without her belt. After the lift she discovered that she was not wearing her belt. Also in the bench press, a woman's lift was turned down, but she didn't seem to hear the head judge. She had elevated her heel during the lift. From much farther away, I heard him, clearly, as he declared, "No good. You lifted your foot." She came off the bench with a big smile, which quickly turned to a look of dismay as her trainer explained what had happened.

A "blind rage," perhaps the ultimate of arousal, is just that—blind. The more that you need to "see" in order to perform well, the farther below the level of rage your arousal needs to be.

I have discussed at length, so far in the present chapter, techniques of centering and of charging. As important as these are for the lifter, they are an incomplete sequence, bioenergetically speaking. Two additional elements are required, namely, "grounding" and "discharging."

No matter how centered one is in her or his embodiment in the here-and-now, and how optimally charged, one will not be able to lift well without good grounding. "Grounding" means contact with the literal, physical ground. It means being planted in such a manner that one has solid support for the task about to be done. The more solidly grounded one is, the more energy one can direct and manage. Grounding affords stability.

The issue of grounding adds a complexity to the already complex issue of optimal arousal. There is an intimate relationship between charging and grounding. A lack of adequate grounding will undermine the effectiveness of what would under circumstances of good grounding be an optimal charge.

Turning, now, to practicalities, I want to address techniques of grounding for the lifter. It doesn't take a lot of words, or complex words to describe the process of grounding. I do suggest that you not be misled by its simplicity, and that you practice it well. Since we all do work with grounding, it is tempting to overlook it. But, in our everyday lives we take it for granted, and do it mostly outside our awareness. So, I propose the following experiment:

> Stand bare footed on a smooth, solid, hard surface. Unlock your knees and place your feet in a comfortable position, about shoulder width. Close your eyes and breathe comfortably. Feel the floor under you. Wiggle your toes. Explore the floor with your toes, leaving your feet in place. Shift your weight to the balls of your feet. Shift your weight back on your heels. Shift your weight from one foot to the other. Bend your knees slightly and let your energy "sink" down into your lower body, all the way to the floor.

If you do this experiment very slowly, and with close awareness, you will experience what is meant by being grounded. You may recognize the sensation, and realize that it has close kinship with being centered. In fact, centering and grounding techniques can be used together to deal with an overcharge of energy.

In the standing position, grounding is through the legs and feet. It is these body parts which connect one with the earth. When one is in other positions, other body parts which are in contact with some solid, supporting surface may become primary. In sitting on a stool with one's feet on the floor, for instance, one may ground through one's feet, legs, and buttocks. By lifting one's feet one can feel how much less grounded one becomes, using the buttocks alone.

In addition to the primary grounding that involves the contact boundary between the physical body and the actual physical ground, there can be a secondary grounding through the eyes. Looking intently at a stationary object anchors one in the actual physical world. The ballet dancer learns when doing a pirouette to look at some single stationary point as he or she passes that point on each rotation. This gives a moment of greater stability in an otherwise and intentionally rather weakly grounded situation.

Just as one lifts or poses better from a centered position and from a position of optimal charge, one will lift or pose better from a well-grounded position. For this reason I will describe grounding techniques for specific lifting situations. All of these are but variations on the above exercise.

The following instructions are general directions for grounding in preparation for any standing lift. Since one is getting grounded in the presence of the bar, this can be referred to as "addressing the bar." Before addressing the bar, appropriate centering and charging have been done.

> Walk to the bar and place your feet at the width that feels most supportive and stable, and at a distance from the bar which gives you the best leverage. Take time to move your feet until the position feels just right. Bend your knees slightly and **feel** the floor under you. Shift your weight more to one foot, then to the other. Equalize your weight between your two feet. Let your energy "sink" into your legs and feet. **Feel** your energy flow smoothly and powerfully up and down your body, connecting your whole body from feet to hands. Look at the bar intently. Bend your knees, bend down and place your hands exactly at the width that you know to be most comfortable for this lift. **Feel** the hard steel in your firm grip.

From this point, the task is to execute one's technique with an appropriate amount of force. The above instructions are a model. The individual lifter can practice this model and make any personal modifi-cations which he or she sees fit to make.

The grounding sequence must be quick, or else one may begin to lose the optimal charge one has built. With practice, grounding can be done in only a few seconds. **In actual practice one may ground and charge at the same time.** Learn to do each by itself, then you can experiment with combining them. In competition, I do some charging before ad-dressing the bar. As I am planting my feet I take three to five huge, loud, forced thoracic breaths through my mouth, thus running my charge up to the optimal level. Then I grasp the bar, spending no more than a cou-ple seconds, exhale completely, take one huge thoracic breath, and lift. I find that in practice, unless I am attempting a limit or near limit lift, I do all the charging I need as I am addressing the bar.

When bench pressing, grounding is through the upper back, the but-tocks, and the feet. So, plant your feet well. While lifting, push against the floor with your feet. Never lift your feet or move them while bench pressing. Keep them firmly planted. (The exception is when, for exer-cise purposes, some lifters put their feet on the bench itself, or even stick their legs into the air. This is intentionally ungrounding in order to make the exercise more difficult.) Wiggle on the bench until you feel well planted in your buttocks and your upper back.

On the incline bench, again, it is crucial to get your feet well planted. Push with your legs to get the needed stability. Get your buttocks and back planted firmly on the bench.

When sitting, grounding will be primarily through the legs and feet and the buttocks. Keep the feet firmly planted and push with the legs enough to insure stability.

Exercise machines present special problems in grounding. Designed to isolate a given muscle group, they often put one in an inefficient posi-tion with respect to grounding oneself. For this reason some machines have belts for strapping oneself in place. Before lifting on any machine, get stabilized as best you can. Whatever part of your body is bearing the major part of your bodyweight is the part to "sink" your energy into, and thus anchor yourself. Of course, the machines are not meant for max-imal lifts; they are meant for exercising relatively isolated muscle groups without full assistance from other muscles.

In competitive lifts which have two phases, there are two occasions for grounding. In the squat one needs to be well grounded before taking the bar off the rack, and again before actually executing the squat. In the clean and jerk one needs to ground before the clean, and ground again before executing the jerk. And in that most awkward of all competitive lifts, the snatch, there are really two phases. This is especially true in the squat style. One obviously needs to ground before starting the snatch. Less often acknowledged is that when in the squat position with a heavily loaded bar held over head at arms length, one again needs to get well grounded in order to recover to the standing position.

The simple fact is that if one is not grounded before lifting a weight, he or she will lose balance and lose leverage in the attempt to find her or his grounding. In the most dramatic scenario, the ungrounded lifter finds herself or himself abruptly and painfully grounded by the unforgiving demand of gravity.

The final task of the body as an energetic system is to discharge. Once the lifter is centered, appropriately charged, and grounded, what remains is to discharge her or his energy. The force of that discharge is measured by the amount of weight lifted. **The discharge is focused by virtue of the lifter's centeredness and grounding. Its forcefulness is a reflection of the lifter's muscular strength and level of chargedness.**

Maximal muscular effort is supported by the forceful, full, thoracic exhalation. The challenge is not to exhale so quickly that the lift is not completed by the end of the breath. One cannot maintain the maximal level of muscular effort while sucking in the next breath. For this reason, the heavy lift is usually begun with the breath held after a huge thoracic inhalation. If the lifting time is short, as in a speed lift such as a clean, a jerk, or a snatch, the breath may be held until the bar is locked out, and then the lifter exhales forcibly. For lifts which take longer, such as a press, bench press, squat, or deadlift, there is the danger of holding the breath too long and getting dizzy or even losing consciousness. Therefore, the exhalation begins during the lift. But it must be timed such that its completion does not precede the completion of the lift.

In performing exercise lifts, the guideline is to exhale during the effort phase of the exercise. With the light to moderate weights used in most exercises, it is not necessary to hold one's breath. Sometimes, however, as one approaches the end of a set, it may be necessary to hold one's breath for the first part of a repetition or two.

Being centered at the time of discharge means being at one with the task. No distractions. No ambivalence. No hesitation. No holding back. The discharge is the explosion of one's commitment. So, upon discharge, one puts every bit of available energy into the lift. Precise and narrow is the focus of energy.

The lifter is a living energy system. Viewed bioenergetically, the lifter's tasks are to charge, ground, and discharge. These energetic tasks are managed by means of a state of centeredness. This perspective is depicted in Figure 13. This is the lifter's sequence for success.

Figure 13

Center, Charge, Ground, Discharge

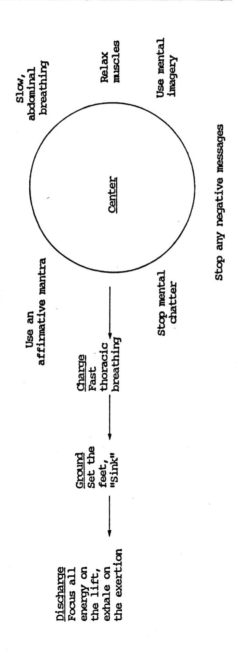

For the posing performance the sequence is basically the same. Centering is exactly the same. Charging is done in the same manner, but not to as high a state of arousal as for heavy lifting. Grounding must be done with each pose struck, but as smoothly and unobtrusively as possible. The discharge is through the exhalation and muscle tensing of each pose which is struck. A posing routine, then, becomes a series of charging, grounding, and discharging sequences, as one flows from pose to pose.

Chapter 10

THE "LIFTING TRANCE"

BEFORE EXPLORING the lifting trance, I suggest that you, the reader, be thoroughly acquainted and adept with the methods already presented. Be able to quiet any unwanted mental chatter, relax any muscles held in tension, and stop any voice of an internal critic, at will. Know how to use a mantra and positive visual and kinesthetic imagery for lifting or posing preparation and rehearsal, as well as rehearsal through the enactment of fantasy. Master the deep, slow, intentional, diaphragmatic breathing which is used for centering, and the fast, forced, costal breathing used for charging. Become adept at grounding, quickly and solidly, and regulating your level of charge, keeping it at an optimal level for your exercise, your lift, or your pose. These are extremely powerful psychological techniques. To benefit from them to the utmost, practice them well and frequently. When you have become proficient with these, you are ready to explore lifting while in a trance.

When I write of a trance state, I am referring to a state that is similar to being centered, but even more so. It is a "hyper-centered" state in which one can manage a high charge of energy, and focus one's discharge like a laser beam. In the lifting trance, energy does not leak out; there are no distractions from the singleness of purpose. The purpose, of course, is the exactly focused explosive discharge. In physique work, it is hitting the pose with everything you have. In lifting a truly heavy weight, it is exploding with everything you have, in the groove of that lift. In exercising, it is staying in each repetition, one by one, until the set is complete, putting as much of what you have into each set as you choose.

From what I have just written, it is apparent that the primary value of lifting in a trance is to bring about an optimal discharge. It allows for the convergence of all of one's organismic resources in that moment of

145

expressed energy. Anecdotes abound which are folk evidence of the immense personal strength which **can** be tapped in crisis evoked trance
states. We have all heard of the physically frail woman who swam
against the flood tides to rescue her child, or the man who lifted the back
end of a car so that an injured person could be pulled from underneath
it. Such stories make exciting telling as well as hearing, and may be subject to exaggeration as they are told and retold. But, even taking into account such growing with the retelling of the tale, there is ample
anecdotal evidence of this phenomenon of unusual physical ability. In
sports, too, this is well-known. Several fascinating examples are provided by Murphy and White (1978) in *The Psychic Side of Sports*. And, interestingly, these authors mention that many athletes report performing
in a "playing trance."

In the yoga tradition, there is evidence for the development of
"siddhis," powers which go beyond what are the expected normal mechanical capacities. And, central to the development of siddhi is pranayama, or the control of "prana," the life force. Since the external
manifestation of prana is the breath, pranayama practice involves
breathing exercises. Some of the techniques of pranayama are far more
complex than the breathing techniques which I have presented for centering and for charging.

Both Eastern and Western disciplines demonstrate, in common, certain practices for the development of exceptional performances. And,
**even though the specific methods differ in some respects, the prac-
tices consist of relaxation, breathing exercises, emptying the mind
of chatter, rhythmic activity, and concentration.** Note that we have
covered, already, three of the five practices. These practices prepare one
for entering a state of trance by eliminating the distractions. After this
preparation, the two other methods — rhythmic activity and
concentration — can usher one ahead, into a state of trance.

The lifting trance need not be a deep trance. The deepest states of
trance tend to take one out of active contact with the physical world, and
are therefore not suitable for lifting. Since a deep trance is not required
by the lifter, he or she does not have to be concerned with creating optimal trance inducing conditions. The rhythmic activity mentioned above
is often time-consuming. When a truly profound trance state is sought,
the seeker may be eager to spend considerable time chanting, dancing,
rocking, whirling or whatever. Most of these rhythmic activities are not
very practical for the lifter. A modicum of rhythmic activity can, however, be experienced by the lifter during both breathing for centering

and breathing for charging. In addition, the lifter may get involved in the rhythm of her or his chanting of a mantra. But, in general, the lifter need not be concerned with any extended involvement with rhythmic activity for producing the lifting trance.

The trance state is an altered state of consciousness (ASC). We need to be clear about what is meant by an altered state of consciousness. The ASC can be defined as any mental state which can be recognized subjectively by the person herself or himself, or objectively by an observer, as being **a significant deviation in subjective experience or psychological functioning** from what is the general norm for that person during alert, waking consciousness (Ludwig, 1969). So, the ASC can range from a mild alteration in the usual alert, waking state to a profound shift in that state. And, although the alteration can be ushered in by means of various physiological and psychological maneuvers and by means of various drugs, only those means which do not interfere with lifting are of value to the lifter.

What happens when an ASC is induced? It appears that **there is an optimal range of stimulation from the outside world which is necessary for maintaining normal, waking consciousness.** It is as if the sensory system is constantly scanning the environment in order to stay oriented. **When the level of stimulation is either greater or less than the optimal level, an ASC can ensue.** An altered state can also be produced by certain types of interference with the normal outflow of motor impulses, the normal emotional tone, or the normal organization of cognitive processes. These methods, however, are of less importance to the lifter in pursuit of the lifting trance.

Another related term for us to be clear about is, of course, "hypnosis." The term "hypnosis" is sometimes used interchangeably with the term "trance." The two terms are, more accurately, not synonyms. The clearest and most useful definition of hypnosis which I know was offered by Ron Shor (1969). Without getting too far in depth, I want to give an overview of his theory. Hypnosis involves three independent dimensions. In any given instance of hypnosis, the subject reaches a particular depth along each of the dimensions. The first dimension is that of "trance," or the extent to which the generalized, everyday, reality orientation has faded into unawareness. The second dimension of hypnosis involves the depth to which the subject enacts the role which he or she believes is the way a hypnotized person would act. This dimension is that of "role-taking." And, third, is the dimension which Shor called "archaic involvement," meaning the extent to which the subject becomes as an obedient child, relating to the hypnotist as a powerful parent figure. Since these three dimensions of hypnosis are independent, and, therefore, depth of trance, depth of role-taking, and depth of archaic involvement can all vary from shallow to profound, there are many varieties of hypnotic experience.

As Shor's theory shows, then, **hypnosis is a particular form of trance, which involves a degree of culturally influenced role-enactment and of regressive involvement.**

Some people speak of "autohypnosis," or hypnosis in which a person hypnotizes herself or himself. Autohypnosis involves the same procedures which the society has defined as hypnotic procedures, but without the external hypnotist.

The terminology is important for understanding what various writers mean when they use these several related concepts. Remember, "altered state of consciousness" (ASC) or "trance" is the broader concept, while "hypnosis" refers to a certain set of phenomena involving an ASC.

The secret which I wish to reveal is the secret of the creation of the lifting trance. Already, I have given a hint. A few paragraphs back, I spoke of the need for a constant sensory scanning of the environment in order to maintain the usual reality orientation. Without that, one slips easily into the non-ordinary reality of the altered state. So, in order to create the lifting trance, one must stop the sensory scanning. This is done by focusing on one thing only — the here-and-now moment. I will come back to this, in more specific detail in a few moments.

It is pointed out in the hypnosis literature that most techniques of induction involve suggestions of **relaxation** and of **concentration** (London, 1967). We have already explored, in previous chapters, the importance of relaxation for the lifter, and methods for bringing it about. Our task, now, is to explore and come to an understanding of concentration.

The usual waking sensory scanning process keeps us oriented to a composite experience of our environment. By scanning, we use a sweeping focus, a focus which moves from thing to thing, perhaps pausing here and there, then moving on. There is a constant integration of this sound, that sight, this smell, that tactile sensation, and so on. These form a composite orienting experience. If, however, we stop scanning, and concentrate more narrowly, on one thing, our composite experience is traded for an ingredient experience. Erving Polster (1970), a master Gestalt therapist, has observed that when these ingredient experiences, which are frequently unattended, are explored, one may develop a heightened experience. This focus on an ingredient experience is known as concentration. Concentration involves giving very close regard to the specific object of one's interest. It is clearly and specifically focusing one's full attention. Polster relates the use of concentration to hypnosis. Furthermore, he notes that this use of concentration holds an advantage over some other methods of inducing an altered state. Namely, with concentration, one may quickly and easily return to the ordinary reality. A quick movement or a sharp sound in the environment can be detected, and one can return to a sensory scan, to the composite experience of one's world. The advantage of this ease of movement from trance to non-trance state for the lifter is obvious. The lifter can stay closely enough in touch with what is going on around her or him to be able to respond to changing circumstances, while still having the benefit of lifting in a state of trance.

The key to the lifting trance is concentration. The one and only Arnold alluded to this in his autobiography when he wrote, "I knew the secret: Concentrate..." (Schwarzenegger, 1977, p. 89).

What does it mean to "concentrate?" Literally, it means to be with a center, to get right into the center of a situation — "con centrum." This requires an absence of tension. Concentration is relaxed, yet purposeful. It is not a forced attention, but rather a focus arising from genuine interest, even fascination. "Trying" interferes with authentic concentration. If one is trying to concentrate, this is evidence that one is trying to force attention to something in which, at the moment, one is not truly interested. Concentration is a relaxed state.

To concentrate, then, one narrows one's attention in both time and space. One focuses attention on what is here-and-now. And, one keeps one's focus on a narrow aspect of the here-and-now, when one wants to enter a state of trance.

Let me offer some concrete guidelines for you to follow in order to create a lifting trance. Assume, first, that all prior conditions have been met. One is well-centered, adequately charged, and well-grounded. The very act of centering, charging and grounding, when well done, will carry one to the door of an altered reality. Now, only a small step is required to pass through that door and into a state of trance. That step is **exquisite concentration on the present moment.** My way of taking that step is as follows, as I have just addressed the bar:

> I look off at a distance, at some irrelevant point. As I do so, I allow my peripheral vision to blur and fade. At the same time I allow all sounds outside my body to fade to softness. I feel the rush of energy inside, following my last few charging breaths. I shift my vision to the bar, and

see the bar as a vivid, outstanding figure. For a moment, I see the bar ever so clearly. It seems to almost glow against a very faded background of sights and sounds. For a moment nothing exists except the bar and me! **I have no thoughts. All that exists is the-bar-and-me in a timeless moment.**

I pause here, in my writing, to create an artificial transition. What I have just described is my own style of inducing my lifting trance. This is **the induction.** As I lift, I then lift in a trance. That is **the use of an established state of trance.** Before continuing the sharing of my personal experience of lifting in trance, I want to present some theoretical material on the established ASC.

There are some differences in ASCs, both as observed from outside and as subjectively reported. In spite of such objective and subjective differences, there are, however, a number of characteristics which are present to a greater or lesser degree in any ASC (Ludwig, 1969). Let me mention each of these, briefly:

(1) Alterations in thinking. (Changes in concentration, attention, memory and judgment. Primitive modes of thought may predominate. Incongruities may coexist without logical conflict.)

(2) Disturbed time sense. (Time may be accelerated or slowed down, as if to stand still.)

(3) Loss of control. (Paradoxically, the person may have a sense of giving up ordinary control in order to gain a more desired level of control or power.)

(4) Change in emotional expression. (There may be either a sense of emotional detachment, or the experience of emotional extremes.)

(5) Body image change. (Body parts may feel shrunken, enlarged, distorted, heavy, or weightless. Blurring of vision, dizziness, numbness, tingling are possible. The boundary between self and the world may dissolve.)

(6) Perceptual distortions. (Perception may seem especially acute. Hallucinations can occur.)

(7) Change in meaning or significance. (A "eureka" experience, a sense of great insight, illumination, understanding and truth.)

(8) Sense of the ineffable. (An inability to communicate or share the nature or essence of the experience, because of the uniqueness of that subjective experience.)

(9) Feelings of rejuvenation. (A sense of overall well-being, hope, or "rebirth.")

(10) Hypersuggestibility. (Increased susceptibility to respond to suggestions from others or to respond to cues from the environment.)

As I indicated, these are the several common characteristics of all ASCs. In any particular ASC one may find any combination of these in greater or lesser evidence.

What about the lifting trance, that specific ASC which is of most interest to those in the world of iron? I know of no systematic research on the specific profile of characteristics found in the lifting trance. I can, however, relate to the above mentioned trance characteristics through my own experience with the lifting trance. I will take the trance characteristics one by one.

The alteration in thinking which I have experienced has involved a virtual cessation of thought, while in the lifting trance. My concentration has been so focused on the here-and-now moment, that I had neither active memories, nor active anticipations of what has been to come. Time has stood still. The loss of control has been the loss of a sense of ego, a sense that "I" was not lifting, but more like "lifting was being done" almost in spite of "me." Along with this loss of a sense of a controlling ego, has been a sense of "detached well-being." All has seemed right with the world. In my times of most profound trance, I have had a sense of weightlessness. It has been as if the bar and I fairly floated together. The world and I have been one, such that, as I said, little sense of a separate "I" even existed. My vision has blurred, almost as if I have been looking under water. I have felt little or no pain, even at times of injuring myself. I have dropped a weight on myself, feeling little, and banged my knee on the platform in a split style snatch, without pain. The pain came later, after I had come out of the lifting trance. The world has seemed simple and right. The experience of lifting heavy weights while in a trance has seemed beyond possible description. It must be experienced to be known. Lifting at the referee's signal has at times seemed automatic, as if I had no choice. It has been as if I have taken his "suggestion" to lift, without thought or real choice. And, finally, in the moment of successful completion of a heavy lift, I have had an exhilaration beyond description. Times of heavy lifting in a state of trance have been some of my peak experiences. The sense of rebirth has stayed with me for some time, only gradually fading over the course of several days.

Now, I want to continue my phenomenological description of the experience of establishing and lifting in the lifting trance, which I interrupted a few paragraphs ago. Return with me to the lifting platform.

> I grasp the bar. One full exhalation, loud against the silence. One huge breath. A rush of energy — tingling all over. The bar-and-I are happening! We are moving! The bar is floating up, along an invisible, but

clearly felt groove. The bar feels heavy and yet floating, at the same time. I am fascinated with this sensation. It seems uncanny. Heavy and weightless, at the same time! Time has become strange. This seems like only a moment, and yet it seems like it is going on and on. This rapid yet endless moment is all that matters. Everything except the bar-and-I is a very dim background. Everything seems right. The bar-and-I lock out. I am breathing hard. My world begins to open up and let in more from outside. I see the referee. I hear him say "It's good!" Yes, yes, he is so right! All is good! And right, and as it should be! I guide the bar back on its crashing return to the platform. The sound echoes and I feel the reverberations of the crash in the boards of the platform. I hear the applause and cheers from the audience. I smile all over. I glow! I feel wonderful! I feel exhilarated! I walk off the platform with a sense of awe, a sense that I have just been a part of the Mystery.

What I have described is my peak experience with the lifting trance. Of course, this does not happen every time I go into a lifting trance. My trance state varies in depth, from quite profound in this example from competition, to rather light, as I sometimes use in a workout. Consistent with the psychological research, I have found that with practice I have learned to induce my trance more and more quickly and easily. In a workout, for instance, I may induce a light trance before several of my sets, and do this in a matter of seconds, while I am centering, charging, and grounding. These several processes overlap for me, and are usually quite rapid. Sometimes, in fact, when I am lifting alone, even in a gym, I spontaneously go into a trance as I address a barbell. At those times when I am lifting near my limit, and especially in competition, I take more time to carefully center, charge, ground, and induce my lifting trance.

Again, I want to emphasize that my description of my lifting trance is from my experience. Your experience will be different in some respects. **Each person's lifting trance is a unique experience.** I have discussed the common elements of trance states, and given an example of my lifting trance. Each person's will be different.

It may be useful for you to practice acts of concentration so as to become very familiar with the feel of slipping smoothly into a trance. To begin this practice, work in a setting where there is a minimum of distraction. Try the following experiment:

> Sit comfortably in a quiet, private place. Breathe abdominally, slowly and rhythmically. Look at some object which is about eye level and somewhere between four and ten feet away. Gaze at that object, constantly. If your gaze drifts away, gently bring it back, once again, to that object. Do not stare. Any forcing will detract from your relaxed

concentration. Allow your thoughts to come to quiet. Again, do not try to force your thoughts away, as such forcing will, itself, pre-empt concentration. If thoughts come, simply let go of them. Do not intentially think of them, and do not try not to think of them. Simply let go. Allow them to drift on by, like a cloud in the sky. In a few minutes, you will experience a trance. Do not be afraid. There is no danger. If you become afraid, the trance will fade, as you come to focus on the experience of being afraid. Just relax, and concentrate. Enjoy the experience of being in trance, as you become more and more familiar with it. You can come back to your ordinary state of consciousness at any time by simply shifting your gaze off the object of your concentration.

When you get to the point that you can enter a trance state rather quickly and predictably, say within a matter of a few seconds, you are ready for the next step. The next step in developing your concentration is to learn to concentrate even in the presence of distractions. Practice relaxed concentration, as you did before, but with increasing levels of distraction. Do not rush your progress. Master each level of distraction before moving to a level of even greater distraction. For distraction, you can play music, with increasing volume. You can have a television set with picture and sound, the video display being near your object of concentration. You can practice while sitting in a crowd at a concert or sporting event. Keep practicing relaxed concentration in various settings offering various modes of distraction (visual, auditory, tactile), until you can concentrate well enough to enter into an altered state of consciousness in the gym and in competition. And, practice using not only a visual object as your focus of concentration, but a sound, a tactile sensation, and a kinesthetic sensation. As each of these is the focus of your concentration, all other stimulation within that mode (visual, auditory, tactile, kinesthetic) and all of the stimulation from the other modes is to be selectively inattended.

What this means is that the lifter can learn to induce a lifting trance by concentrating not only on a visual object, but by concentrating on a sound, a tactile sensation, or a kinesthetic sensation. For example, a tapping on the knee might be the tactile sensation of focus. Or, the kinesthetic sensations of pumping out a set of curls could become the focus. My personal preference for creating a lifting trance has been, however, a visual focus of concentration.

It is a basic law of perception that a person can fully attend to only one thing at a time. Concentration is exclusive — it excludes all but the object of concentration. The illusion of attending to more than one thing at a time is created by rapidly shuttling from attending to one thing, then to the other. This split consciousness drastically reduces concentration. As one shifts from an exclusive focus of attention to shuttling between two or among more than two stimuli, one is getting away from the trance inducing concentration and back to the scanning behavior which is the anchor to ordinary reality. Remember, it is complete, sustained concentration that will open the door to the state of lifting trance.

When you have mastered the creation of the lifting trance, you will lift, at times, as if in a dream. Learning to lift in a trance is, indeed, training in the art of self-forgetfulness. Selfless, ego-less, the dance of power happens. Nothing exists but the immediate experience of being in the center of that dance. Flesh and iron move as one, creating its own esthetic in motion. Suddenly, the whole experience can disintegrate. Or, it can become complete. This is the flow of total involvement, the dance which is transcendent. In posing, the dance may last longer and be easier to recognize from outside.

Ecstasy, known as a mystic or poetic trance, comes to the lifter who has mastered the lifting trance. To some, it is known that periodic plunges into ecstasy bring a transformation to one's ordinary consciousness. So, chalk your hands, and concentrate. This is meditation in the world of iron.

REFERENCES

Allport, G.: *Pattern and Growth in Personality.* New York, Holt, Rinehart and Winston, 1961.

Castaneda, C.: *The Teachings of Don Juan: A Yaqui Way of Knowledge.* New York, Ballantine, 1968.

Coffin, R.: *Poetry for Crazy Cowboys and Zen Monks.* Santa Barbara, California, Ross-Erikson, 1980.

Gaines, C. and Butler, G.: *Pumping Iron: The Art and Sport of Bodybuilding.* New York, Simon and Schuster, 1974.

Gallwey, W.: *The Inner Game of Tennis.* New York, Bantam, 1974.

Gallwey, T. and Friegel, B.: *Inner Skiing.* New York, Bantam, 1977.

Gaudreau, L.: *Anvils, Horseshoes and Cannons: The History of Strongmen, Vol. 1.* Self-published, 1975.

Hall, C. and Lindzey, G.: *Theories of Personality.* New York, John Wiley, 1970.

Herrigel, E.: *Zen in the Art of Archery.* New York, Vintage, 1953.

Jacobson, E.: *Progressive Relaxation.* Chicago, University of Chicago Press, 1938.

Jones, A.: The history and development of Nautilus. In Riley, D. (Ed.): *Strength Training by the Experts.* West Point, N.Y., Leisure Press, 1977.

Jung, C.: *The Archetypes and the Collective Unconscious.* Princeton, Princeton University Press, 1968.

Jung, C.: *Civilization in Transition.* Princeton, New Jersey, Princeton University, 1970.

Keen, S.: The cosmic versus the rational. *Psychology Today, 8,* 2 (July), 56-59, 1974.

Leonard, G.: *The Ultimate Athlete.* New York, Avon, 1974, 1975.

London, P.: The induction of hypnosis. In Gordon, J.: *Handbook of Clinical and Experimental Hypnosis.* New York, Macmillan, 1967.

Ludwig, A.: Altered states of consciousness. In Tart, C.: *Altered States of Consciousness.* New York, Wiley, 1969.

Maslow, A.: *Toward a Psychology of Being,* 2nd ed. New York, Von Nostrand Reinhold, 1968.

McCluggage, D.: *The Centered Skier.* New York, Warner, 1977.

Murphy, M.: *Golf in the Kingdom.* New York, Dell, 1972.

Murphy, M. and White, R.: *The Psychic Side of Sports.* Reading, Addison-Wesley, 1978.

Pearl, B.: *Keys to the Inner Universe.* Pasadena, California, Physical Fitness Architects, 1978.

Pirsig, R.: *Zen and the Art of Motorcycle Maintenance.* New York, William Morrow, 1974.

Polster, E.: Sensory functioning in psychotherapy. In Fagan, J. and Shepherd, I.: *Gestalt Therapy Now.* Palo Alto, California, Science and Behavior Books, 1970.

Rasch, P.: *Weight Training.* Dubuque, Wm. C. Brown, 1966.

Ravizza, K.: Peak experiences in sport. *Journal of Humanistic Psychology, 17,* 4, 35-40, 1977.

Reich, W.: *Character Analysis.* New York, Noonday, 1949.

Riley, D.: Strength training equipment. In Riley, D. (Ed.): *Strength Training by the Experts.* West Point, N.Y., Leisure Press, 1977.

Rohé, F.: *The Zen of Running.* New York, Random House, 1974.

Schwarzenegger, A.: *Arnold: The Education of a Bodybuilder.* New York, Simon and Schuster, 1977.

Shor, R.: Three dimensions of hypnotic depth. In Tart, C.: *Altered States of Consciousness.* New York, John Wiley, 1969.

Shostrom, E.: *Man, the Manipulator.* Nashville, Tennessee, Abingdon, 1967.

Smith, E.: In praise of the curl for arm development. *Iron Man, 44,* 3, March, 1985.

Smith, E.: *The Body in Psychotherapy.* Jefferson, N.C., McFarland, 1985.

Spino, M.: *Beyond Jogging.* Millbreae, Celestial Arts, 1976.

Todd, T.: *Inside Powerlifting.* Chicago, Contemporary Books, 1978.

Tohei, K.: *Aikido in Daily Life.* Tokyo, Rikugei, 1966.

Tucker, L.: Effect of a weight-training program on the self-concepts of college males. *Perceptual and Motor Skills, 54,* 1055-1061, 1982.

Tucker, L.: Effect of weight-training on self-concept: a profile of those influenced most. *Research Quarterly for Exercise and Sport, 54,* 4, 389-397, 1983.

Willoughby, D. and Weaver, G.: *The Complete Guide to Muscular Measurements.* Weider, 1947.

INDEX

157

Chatter, internal, 111, 113-119, fig. 119, 126, 130, 131, 146
  quieting, 112, 113, 118-120, 126, 145, 146
Chatter, mental (*see* Chatter, internal)
Classical orientation, 69, 70
Coffin, Raymond, 81
Collective unconscious, 36, 41, 88
Compensation, 42
Competition
  bodybuilding, 86, 87
  judging, 11
  lifting, 10, 11, 23
  losers in, 89
  negative effects, 89
  symbolism, 88, 89
  training, 7, 87
  value of, 90, 91
  winners in, 89, 91
  women in, 11
Compulsion, 19
Concentration, 146, 148, 149, 152, 153, 154
  method, 149, 150, 153
Contraction of muscle, 20
Cosmic view, 70
Critic, internal, 115-121, 126, 145
  counter messages, 117-121, 126, 145
  effect, 115-119
Criticism of weight sports, 93-108
  Legitimate, 93-96
  hype, 93, 94, 95
  overstated equipment claims, 94, 95
  overstated product claims, 94, 95
  substandard contests, 94
  undertrained instructors, 95, 96
  Illegitimate, 96-108
  athletes are "dumb," 102
  bodybuilding not a sport, 103
  cardiovascular conditioning, 100, 101
  emotional plague, 107, 108
  ignorance of sport, 93
  misunderstanding, 93
  media generated views, 97
  muscle bound, fear of, 98, 99, 100
  narcissism, 102
  psychological reaction, negative, 105-108
  sports versus athletics, 103, 104
  uselessness of strong muscles, 101
  esthetics, 97, 98

D

Demosthenes, 42
Desensitization, 28, 29, 30
Dialogue, internal, 23
Diet (*see* Nutrition)
Dionysian orientation, 67-70, 73-77
Discharging, 129, 134, 142, 143, fig. 143, 145
Discipline, 17, 18, 19, 20, 45, 51, 54, 55, 83
Distractions, eliminating, 146
Dumbbells (*see* equipment)

E

Egotism, 102
Emotional plague, 107, 108
Energy overcharge, 103, 136-139
Enhancement of lifting
  lifting trance, 149-151
  psychological, 111
  techniques, 111
Equipment
  barbells, 61, 62, 63, 64, 67
  development, 60, 61, 62, 63, 64
  dumbbells, 61, 62, 63, 64, 65, 67
  free-weights, 59, 64, 66, 67
  machines
    high-tech, 59, 60, 64, 65, 67, 74, 141
    isokinetic, 65
    pulley, 64
  Nautilus, 65, 66, 67
  preference, psychological, 67
  purpose, 59, 61
  standardized, 62, 63
Eros principle, 69, 73
Exercise parameters
  coordination, 35, 36, 100, 101
  endurance, 35, 36, 100, 101, 104
  flexibility, 35, 100, 101
  speed, 35, 36, 100, 101
  strength, 35, 36, 59, 100, 101, 104
Existence, parameters, 129
Extension of muscle, 20, 83

F

Feminine qualities, 21, 69, 72, 106
Flexibility, 20, 99, 100
Freud, S., 41